Elite College Application Essays

(Second Edition)

COLLECTED AND EDITED BY THE STAFF OF

THE EAST COAST COLLEGE FORUM

ACKNOWLEDGEMENTS

We would like to thank the hundreds of brilliant students who submitted their essays for consideration. With only the knowledge that their experience might benefit others in return, they provided invaluable help.

Thanks to Miss. Jennifer Lu for the timely article of "Seven Tips on College Essays".

Special appreciation goes to Mr. Yunshi Wang, for his inspiring article. His unique point of view is thought provoking.

We also would like to thank Dr. Leila Sevigny for her wise advice and editorial help.

TABLE OF CONTENTS

Preface

Competition, competition, competition!

Competition is indeed the word that reflects the reality in the process of college applications that high school seniors are facing today. Any dream to get into the world's most selective colleges and universities can hardly come true without a decent presentation of a competitive application package. Among the various components of an application package, a well-conceived and well-written personal essay is so critical that it could become a saving grace under many circumstances.

There are plenty of books out there on how to write winning college essays, and ours is not meant to be just another one of them.

In this book, our readers have a bountiful collection of essays written by the most recent high school graduates who have been admitted into the nation's best universities and colleges including Ivy League schools. Our intention is to give our readers a flavor of real and practical personal essays, and at the same time, to demystify the so-called winning essay, which often is overly exaggerated by some guidebooks. Reading through these collected essays should open our readers' minds and give them the power to reflect on their hobbies, passions, personalities and any other qualities that truly tell who they are. As one can expect, an admission officer can only spend a few minutes reading each applicant's essay; and needless to say, to wow them, one should think of crafting an attention grabber to create an "aha" moment. Our advice is to glean the unique perspectives from these successful applicants to tackle the essay topics.

Presenting these timely collected essays, thanks to the essay authors, is our best wish to all the high school seniors in their college application process.

Seven Tips on College Essays

Every spiel is the same. On every college visit, chipper tour guides gush about their school's gothic architecture, close faculty-student relationships, and how they definitely, positively, without a doubt have "the best dining hall food in the country."

After 3-4 (or perhaps 15) of these tours, you've finally decided on your dream college. You can already see yourself pulling all-nighters in the library or playing Ultimate Frisbee on the quad. But before you unpack your dorm room starter kit, you have to, well... get in. That's where the college essay comes in. Now it's your turn to sell yourself to colleges – but what do you have to say?

In honor of overenthusiastic tour guides everywhere, here are the Top 7 Tips to Definitely, Positively, Without a Doubt Improve Your College Essay:

1. Focus on the personal, not the academic. The bulk of your college application already tells admissions officers what kind of student you are. The college essay should show what kind of person you are. What concerns keep you up at night? What can you offer to a college, university, or campus? What's your story?

2. Paint a picture of yourself. The college essay isn't a 500-word retelling of your résumé, GPA, or spreadsheet of volunteer hours. It's a story you craft – a narrative to tie together who you are and who you want to be. Let's all breathe a sigh of relief that what you bring to college isn't just your high school transcript, but your sense of humor, secret talents, generosity to friends and strangers, unflagging persistence, and passion to do/fight for what you love, be that a varsity sport, non-profit, or school newspaper. Use the essay(s) to tell a side of you that can't be found elsewhere on your application. How did a transcontinental move shape you as a child? Why do you pour blood, sweat, and tears into an extracurricular? How did you become a semi-professional part-time juggler? Do you devise your own scientific experiments for fun?

3. Think broadly about your experiences. Senior year can be a rollercoaster of stress, nostalgia, excitement, and fear, and that's how it should be. But it's also the time for introspection. Reflect back on the last three, or three and a half years. What classes have you taken, what extracurricular and volunteer efforts have you made? What kind of friend have you been? How do all these different threads come together to form the friendship bracelet (or cheesy metaphor of your choice) that is you? While you won't cover all of these ideas in your essay, this will help you contextualize your specific essay topic within a broader narrative.

4. *Be descriptive and specific.* After some thinking, you finally have your topic! But how do you begin? Think of your essay as a mini action movie (with the introspective interludes of an independent, avant-garde film). Begin with something attention-grabbing, the literary equivalent of a car chase or explosion. It can be some intriguing dialogue, an audacious statement, or anything quirky, funny, or memorable. One tried and true college essay structure is the anecdotal essay — draw your reader in with a punchy, compelling story and then explain it with some backstory and analysis.

5. *Narrate, don't summarize.* All great essays are great in different ways, but all bad essays are bad in the same ways. Don't summarize. Yes, you joined [insert extracurricular] as a freshman, struggled, then worked your way up to become its beloved president. Congratulations, but that tells your reader nothing that can't be found on your résumé. The essay is unique in its ability to take readers inside your mind and into the narrative at hand. Don't summarize your underdog victory at a fencing competition. Narrate it! What split second decisions or thoughts were racing through your mind? What clever fencing move did you use to joust your way to victory? By giving your reader a front row view of your anecdote, you show off your writing skills, and at the same time, make your essay and yourself memorable ones.

6. *Show, don't tell.* Another common mistake is being too obvious about the moral of the story. It's a fine line to walk: while your essay should always include analysis and a "point," it also shouldn't feel like an Aesop's Fable or a Full House episode. If you've done your job right, you won't need to say at the end, "This is how I learned to be a good person or hard-working student." Instead, show it! If your worldview changed radically after a life-altering event, show us how you thought before and after this event. With enough primary sources (your emotions, dialogue, inner or outer monologue), your readers will be able to see for themselves how you've become the person that you are today.

7. *Use your own voice.* Just as the essay should be about you, the essay should sound like you. Don't be afraid to imbue your essay with your unique voice. It's okay to be colloquial— while it should always be well written, the college essay can be more personal than your average class assignment. A friend should be able to read your essay and recognize your voice in it.

The list could go on, but in the end they boil down to these key themes:

1) Discover who you are
2) Write about who you are
3) Write like who you are

It can be a daunting task to "discover who you are" at the tender age of 17 or 18 but don't worry. This won't define you for the next 30 years, or probably even the next four years. College admissions officers don't want to know who you'll be at age 50 —; they want to know who you are now, with all your innate strengths and flaws, whatever they may be.

– Jennifer Lu

Miss. Jennifer Lu is a senior at Yale University who majors in literature. She has been a Production & Design Editor for the Yale Daily News, and she is currently the Photography Editor at The New Journal and a photo intern at New York Observer. She is also the co-director of JEI Livingston Learning Center, NJ.

Elite Universities, You, and Your Essays

An elite university education doesn't matter at all in a person's success—nowadays, you hear a lot of research findings trying to convince you of this theory. Early this year, New York Times columnist Frank Bruni famously noted that among the American-born chief executives of the top 100 companies in the Fortune 500, just about 30 went to an Ivy League school or equally selective college. However, if you narrow down to the Richest-Five list, you will find that every one of them has been admitted to an elite university. Each of the four most recent presidents, Bush, Clinton, Bush, and Obama, has a degree from a HYP university. The current U.S. Supreme Court is monopolized by Harvard and Yale Law School graduates.

Did you notice the word "American-born" in Bruni's observation and wonder why? I suspect that there are a higher percentage of non-American-born chief executives with Ivy-League degrees. Indeed, there is a good reason why immigrants tend to send their kids to medical schools or accounting schools: because a doctor or an accountant needs a degree and a license to practice, and is therefore much less susceptible to prejudices. You can't easily characterize a licensed immigrant doctor with a Johns Hopkins M.D. degree as incompetent. I have been wondering had the German-Jewish immigrant Henry Kissinger, the Polish immigrant Zbigniew Brzezinski, and the Czech-Jewish immigrant Madeleine Albright never been to an elite university, would any of them have become a giant of American international diplomacy? Elaine Chao, the first Asian-American woman in U.S. history to be appointed as a cabinet member, has a degree from Harvard Business School. We also have I.M. Pei, Yoyo Ma, and Jerry Yang, to name a few successful Chinese-Americans with elite university pedigrees.

For immigrant families and their children who are interested in applying to an elite university, this is always a puzzle: what really seals or breaks a deal? I have heard debates about whether to change a child's last name to make it sound Jewish or European to overcome the invisible quota against Asian-American students (i.e. changing Xin to Sheen or Wang to Wayne). I have also pondered the benefit of having my daughter learn fencing, a European sport, since most elite universities have fencing teams that need a steady inflow of applicants who can lunge and coulé skillfully; but most of the discussions center around producing eye-catching essays in the application packages. What shall we write? Shall we emphasize our ethnic identity by writing about achievements in weiqi, Ping-Pong, badminton, the piano; or shall we Kardashianize our mainstream values—volunteering in homeless shelters and nursing homes or playing football and baseball and even golf, for example? Shall we mention that we spend most of our extracurricular time reading books, hence matching the stereotypes of Asian bookworms, or shall we leave the impression of doing anything and everything other than reading books? Why is it that no one plays the guitar in this collection of essays?

There is a consensus as well: extreme in the writing about overcoming adversities is always safe and convincing (I love people from a freedom-deprived, famine-prone country as well as people growing up in a bullet-flying, drug-infested poor neighborhood, the Williams Sisters!) Moderation in the bragging about one's obsession with a scientific pursuit is nearly suicidal and stupid – it's always inspiring to tell people that you started to recognize Mars and Venus before you were liberated from Huggies. Reminiscing about travelling or living in an exotic place, as far as possible, reflects well on you. Quite a few applicants have revealed casually that they lived the first several years of their lives in China – did that remind the admission committees of Einstein, Fermi, or more recently Elon Musk?

I believe that readers shall make their own decisions, but at least they will be enlightened by those wonderful essays and freed from the mystery of the admission process. In the end, writing essays is just a means to express yourselves. The more genuine and unique you sound – whether to expose yourself as a bookworm obsessed with long-dead French and Russian writers or to declare that you are a multi-racial child, an international adoptee, or even transgender – the more you will touch your intended readers, those mysterious people who may or may not decide your future.

Good luck!

– Yunshi Wang

Yunshi Wang is the co-director of the China-U.S. Zero Emission Vehicle Policy Lab and the director of the China Center for Energy and Transportation at the University of California, Davis Institute of Transportation Studies. He has worked as an energy economist with the World Bank and a research fellow at the MIT Sloan School of Management, conducting research on the Chinese economy with Dean Emeritus and Professor Lester Thurow.

Common Application Essay Prompts

The common application essay prompts for 2014 and 2015 are listed below. Each essay that is marked with "Common" in this book was written for one of the following topics.

1. Some students have a background or story that is so central to their identity that they believe their application would be incomplete without it. If this sounds like you, then please share your story.

2. Recount an incident or time when you experienced failure. How did it affect you, and what lessons did you learn?

3. Reflect on a time when you challenged a belief or idea. What prompted you to act? Would you make the same decision again?

4. Describe a place or environment where you are perfectly content. What do you do or experience there, and why is it meaningful to you?

5. Discuss an accomplishment or event, formal or informal, which marked your transition from childhood to adulthood within your culture, community, or family.

CHAPTER 1

Brown University Application Essays

Brown University

Providence, Rhode Island

2015 admission results: 2,580 offers out of 30,397 applicants, 8.5%

2014 admission rate: 8.6%

Signe was admitted to Brown University, Class of 2019.

In second grade, I worked in construction. I knew that dewy grass was proof of fairies, and that they needed a spot to rest their wings before shining lawns with water. So I gathered my tools and worked ceaselessly, at every possible chance, to build houses for those laborers of light.

I ripped grass, tore bark, and plucked mushrooms, fashioning tiny furniture for whomever needed it most. Alas, the most coveted decor required flowers, not from my grandmother's backyard, but from her neighbor's.

I made a game of the crusade, a dance with security. I would scale the stone partition between their kingdoms, and with sleek grace, snatch Ingrid's tulips. This technique worked innumerable times, until I finally found myself face to face with Ingrid, a dead flower in my hand, and a severed stem in her garden.

With her harsh German accent, she smashed my interest in the supernatural. How could fairies exist in a world of possession and anger? At the ripe age of seven, I had learned, quite sadly, that the beautiful was not necessarily the communal. I did not have the right to uproot pretty things to make my world daintier.

When I went crying to Mormor, who had her own gripes with the Holsteins, she coupled reprimand with hope. First, she reminded me of the etiquette behind not vandalizing gardens. Then, she shaped my little hands about a dented tin cup, with illegible measurements strewn across the sides, and told me to fill it with raspberries.

I thought of the times I had not been permitted to pick them, as their thorns would stab my young skin. I thought of the day that I found one lying somewhere on her dewy grass and squished it with two hostile fingers. Their oblong bodies piqued my curiosity, as I couldn't understand their function. They would not decorate my fairy houses; they were big, lumpy, hairy, red tongues of worm-vines, not flowers by any means.

Nonetheless, my tin cup and I ventured to the end of her lawn, to the armed fortress of red dots and brown roots. In a blur, we stormed the castle with the ferocity of ravenous ants in a picnic maze. I ducked, swerved, swiped, and soon my cup was full.

Perhaps my knee bled. Perhaps I got tired. I recall an ominous, thunder-tinged sky sending me back indoors, where I victoriously marched to Mormor and shared my winnings with her.

Dear God, were they wonderful. If you've never had fresh raspberries, I highly suggest them. They taste like moist rebirth.

For years, I anticipated June in my grandmother's backyard, the thrill of its perpetual treasure hunt. I grew taller and learned new methods of manipulating my body through jagged crannies, always adapting in sight of my prize. For years, I foolishly froze August's last harvest. Until, years later, the raspberry bush died.

And Ingrid died. And her house died. My grandmother is the last gardener on her street of brick-faced lawn-less duplexes. Her turf is the final, finite bastion of dew-stained grass, tall trees, and begging-to-be-plucked tulips.

But I will not pick her tulips; they want to live, not wilt to the touch of scissors. I will not mourn the crumbling of my oasis; I will tuck its ashes in my pocket, or let its colors stain my lips.

Thus, I've stained my lips with cloudberries in Norway, marionberries in Oregon, lingonberries in Sweden, stoneberries in Maine. I coyly steal mulberries at busy street corners, even if I'm running late. I have learned that this wild world is full of fruit, and that beneath the thickest spikes are the sweetest berries. I have learned that fruit is from the same cosmic explosion as human skin and is imperishable as morning dew, and that all fruit begs to be tasted.

Signe was admitted to Brown University, Class of 2019.

Why are you drawn to the area(s) of study you indicated in our Member Section, earlier in this application? If you are "undecided" or not sure which Brown concentrations match your interests, consider describing more generally the academic topics or modes of thought that engage you currently. (150 word limit)

I used to love thesauruses. I would eagerly tightrope through the English language, with a birds-eye-view of generalized speech, to pluck perfect synonyms. Smart became scholarly; beauty died in pulchritude. I categorized ceaselessly, until I fell from overview to obscurity. At mouth level, words are as different as humans. I questioned my relationship with "impressive" language. Was great vocabulary an award? A holier-than-thou distinction? No. Words are tools, letting me view myself within a big picture. I scribble sentences daily, yet most of my writing is based upon banal observances. I've written poems about seashells, pennies, and cobblestones by finding the grandiose in the minuscule. The minuscule, which synonyms ignore, always matters. For example, tiny quips about women indicate deep-rooted sexism. To study tone is to study culture, varied views of humanity. As such, I want to seal hot schisms and celebrate seas between people, finding cusps in language.

Where you have lived?

At 6 A.M., a crazed man screams obscenities. He paces towards me, so I hide in the thrust of a mob. In an instant, a booming voice spits me from St. George's terminal, to the boat. Excelsior. Throughout life, I've used the Staten Island ferry, the dilapidated cork of NYC's wined harbor. It's a census of ghosts, overlooked in a society defined by "Fugghedaboudit". Staten Islanders complain about everything: potholes, taxes, bad pizza. The ferries smell like brackish dust. Yet, when the sun melts like a pat of butter over Brooklyn, I cannot help but love my frenzied, forgotten borough.

Communities or Groups

At times, my house has functioned like a hotel. Last month, family from Sweden slept in my room for four days. A few years ago, I woke up to find an Argentinian breakfast spread out beneath my mother's smiling friend from Mendoza. I've set tables for visitors from Turkey to Wisconsin, all of whom bring fascinating tales, so distanced from Staten Island, right to my ears. My borough is diverse, but its diversity breeds flat acknowledgement. We eat from halal carts without knowing why halal meat exists. Yet, when the universe is in your dining room, you must dance with it. I've chatted with a Bolivian performance artist, born without a birth certificate. I learned the rules of chess from my mother's ex-boyfriend, an Italian with a PhD in English literature. I have absorbed gallons of panoramas and I have laughed, sharing my own pulsing thoughts with the whole world.

Why Brown?

I sit for seven periods. I've taken mandatory Calculus, AP World, AP U.S. History, Russian, Robotics, and Computer Aided Design classes. My school sees passion itself as a mandate, not an unquenched will. The brilliant Staten Island Tech is a luxury, but it has too many walls. Its old building is shaped like an open noose, a three-dimensional "U" amidst mapped suburbia. Tech loves structure for the same reason that some governments love prisons. Truthfully, I think that plans are overrated; getting lost is more illuminating. When colleges boast about their rigid pre-law, pre-med, and pre-usefulness programs, I lose interest. Education is not a diploma lodged in the future, but a flow of epiphanies, or a growing circuit of truths. I felt this education at Brown. Its open curriculum requires innovation; it's filled with fetal questions, and devoid of dying answers. As a Brunonian, I could start the day by synthesizing my passions for nutrition and social justice in "Health, Hunger and the Household in Developing Countries" before blissfully losing sleep over "Urban Fictions, 1850-Present". I can't imagine a greater privilege than killing complacency atop College Hill. High school was for sitting. At Brown, I'll be lost enough to leap.

Taylor was admitted to Brown University, Class of 2019.

I grew up in Belleville, Michigan. Never heard of it? Neither have people living fifteen miles away. In a small Midwest suburb like Belleville, there are certain unspoken expectations for life after high school, and most of them don't include college. Here, it's not uncommon for two or more generations to live on the same street. I have friends who are unable to attend college because of the cost, classmates whose only meal of the day is a school provided lunch, and peers for whom school is the only escape from a neglectful or abusive home. While my town is by no means the nicest in the country, and my school may not be well-known, I feel that I have had a very real childhood. I have seen firsthand what a lack of opportunity looks like; it looks like my town. So how has this insignificant, economically challenged Midwest town had such a profound impact me? Growing up in Belleville has taught me a much more valuable lesson than I could ever learn in the classroom – the value of an education.

Though this is the place where I grew up, from a young age I've had very different goals than most of my peers. At a school where the emphasis is placed on graduating high school, not going to college, I am definitely not the typical student at Belleville High School. My friends think I'm "crazy" for taking the course load that I do. I've exhausted all the Advanced Placement courses at my school, skipped two grade levels in math, and taken four years of all core classes. To me, however, it's not "crazy" to challenge myself. Instead of asking why I should take a difficult course, I always ask, "Why not?" The first AP class I ever took was AP U.S. History. For the first two weeks, I was constantly sobbing over the seemingly ridiculous workload and downright cruel tests. However, once I began to learn the information because I found it interesting, and not just because I felt I had to memorize it for a quiz, my grades improved and my stress lessened. Taking that class made me realize, for the first time, how much more valuable knowledge is than a grade on a test. Of course, maintaining a high grade point average is a priority of mine too, but all the A's in the world don't mean anything if nothing was learned in the process of earning them. APUSH is, to this day, my favorite class that I have ever taken. It sparked a desire for knowledge in me that will inspire me for the rest of my life.

Most freshmen in high school don't think about their plans for the rest of their lives; however, I have known that I wanted to leave this area and create a better life for myself for as long as I can remember. While I am a very active member of my school and have a lot of pride for BHS, I have had to work a lot harder to better my educational opportunities. The focus at Belleville is not on kids like me, the focus is to help kids graduate high school. I constantly feel that my needs are second to those who are struggling, and that I'm expected to just "figure it out myself". While I am envious of those students who receive significant guidance throughout high school from teachers, counselors, or advisors, I am not resentful of my school. I understand that I am a minority here, and I am willing to do more of the work independently. Higher education is important enough to me that although I have to work harder, I will continue to pursue my goals. I am excited to attend college this fall not because it is expected of me, but because I truly understand and value the opportunities that education brings.

Allie was admitted to Brown University, Class of 2019.

"Allie, here, go!" And just like that, a pack of teenage boys is sprinting toward me. I freeze. I awkwardly try to maneuver away, but I am trapped. I close my eyes and prepare for the inevitable assault, when a sound of hope breaks my trance. "You've got me, you've got me," a friend calls from behind. I resume breathing and lob the football in his general direction (with both hands, of course). I'm no Superman, but Physical Education is my Kryptonite.

I was born with the worst coordination skills imaginable in a human being. I am a Grinch of clumsiness – It seems I was born with a cerebellum three sizes too small! Moving my limbs is like moving a robot's with a remote control. So the hardest part of my school day is not deriving differential equations or calculating the radius of the earth, but the football game during gym class.

"Ok, fine, we'll take Allie this time." I happily walk to the team captain who was kind enough to allow me to take up a square foot of his field. When a play starts, I wander the field and aimlessly cheer for my friends. It is understood by all that it is unnecessary for a player to cover me. Even if the ball came my way, the odds of my catching it were slim to none.

I was off to my usual wandering start when that boy thrust the leather-bound ball of doom into my arms. The shock on the field was palpable. My clumsy arms hadn't fumbled the ball. I was about to participate in the game! In the end, all I did was freeze and pass the ball back to my teammate. I started back to wandering. But, before I could walk five paces, I had another pack of boys rushing toward me. This time, they were offering high-fives and back-pats. Apparently, my teammate had scored a touchdown after my pass. "This all started with Allie!" the boy exclaimed. Were they poking fun at me? Of course! But I didn't care. I was ecstatic. I was Eli Manning and I had just won Super Bowl XLII. I waved at my adoring fans.

This still remains the sole occasion I made contact with that football on the field. However, I proved something to myself that day. I challenged my own belief that slim chances mean I should not try. I will continue to take life's challenges as another football game. While the chances of me curing cancer or winning a Nobel Prize in physics are slim to none, so were the chances of me catching that football. And, if either are to happen, the boy that passed me that football in gym class will be the first person I thank.

Brown Essay #5

Monica was admitted to Brown University, Class of 2018.

Instructions: The essay demonstrates your ability to write clearly and concisely on a selected topic and helps you distinguish yourself in your own voice. What do you want the readers of your application to know about you apart from courses, grades, and test scores? Choose the option that best helps you answer that question and write an essay of no more than 650 words, using the prompt to inspire and structure your response. Remember: 650 words is your limit, not your goal. Use the full range if you need it, but don't feel obligated to do so. (The application won't accept a response shorter than 250 words.)

– Some students have a background or story that is so central to their identity that they believe their application would be incomplete without it. If this sounds like you, then please share your story.

"So, where are you from?"

The question echoes in my ears. A flood of uncertainty rushes into my mind. I freeze.

This seemingly simple question has become one of the most daunting when meeting new people. Do I answer precisely or vaguely? The long story or the short story?

As the daughter of an active military member, my family and I typically move every few years. However, due to the nature of my father's recent assignments, my family has moved three times in the past four years. Personally, I have attended a different school for each of my four years of high school. For the past year, I have lived in the Netherlands while attending an international school. The experience is incomparable. Immersed in the assorted cultures of my classmates and teachers has expanded my openness to other ideas. Living and learning abroad has introduced a sense of maturity and humbleness required to accept new thoughts. While living in the Netherlands has offered unparalleled opportunities, it also poses questions I rarely had to answer in the United States.

Over my lifetime, I have lived in Florida, Massachusetts, Rhode Island, New York, Virginia, Zuid-Holland (NL), and Limburg (NL). When meeting new people in the Netherlands, one will typically ask where I am from. To avoid an awkwardly lengthy explanation, I resort to simply saying I am from the United States.

However, the inquirer never fails to pry for further details, leaving me victim to yet another attack – hesitation, doubt, fret. And the struggle does not end here.

Following my enlightenment, the inquirer shoots the final question. The lethal question that sends chills of confusion down my spine; every bone aches with a lack of sureness.

"Where do you consider home?"

The toxicity of the question surges through my veins while my brain stumbles to conjure a response. The words, "I don't know," emerge from my lips unskillfully. Before living in the Netherlands, amongst expatriates who often wonder about the origin of their peers, I never grasped the complexity of the question. Every new place I live in grows to feel like home, despite its freshness and every time I move, there is an emptiness in myself, longing for the place I left, similar to homesickness. Yet when posed with a question about where I consider home, I draw a blank. Do I lack a home? Or do I have a surplus of homes?

The words "house" and "home" are not interchangeable from my perspective. My family rarely owns a house due to the nomadic nature of our lifestyles but we try to make each house our home. These houses become our homes, both materially and emotionally. We pack up and ship our belongings along with us wherever and whenever we move. However, we also have to pack up and ship our hearts and memories. The counselor at the school I ended junior year claims "it takes six months to unpack our hearts and six months to pack our hearts."

According to the philosophy, I have had no time in between for the past four years. Despite the hardships and unsettledness that moving brings, one aspect of my life is solid – my family. My two sisters, my mother, and my father have proven to provide the best support system. Our relationships are quite symbiotic in nature; we help each other to overcome emotional obstacles during moves. Essentially, I have learned that my family is my home.

My lack of commitment to a single place allows me to grow to love each place I live without bitterness and constant longing. With superseding adaptive skills I thrive in each new place, never failing to challenge myself with rigorous class schedules in order to achieve my dream career. I am confident that both in my journey through university and in my career in the medical field, my gift of engrossing myself into new and demanding atmospheres will serve as my basis for success.

CHAPTER 2
Columbia University Application Essays

Columbia University

New York, New York

2015 admission results: 2,228 offers out of 36,250 applicants, 6.1%

2014 admission rate: 6.9%

The author of this essay was admitted to Columbia University, Class of 2018.

The landscape was a blur of monuments and hillsides. Only when the driver announced our arrival at the Library of Congress did I hear Robhullah speak across the dark interior. I could barely make out his words. "What?" I kept whispering back, as we stepped into the night. "What did you say?"

That moment was the apex of a frenzied day; Robhullah and I had spent the earlier hours in preparation. He arranged his paintings until an entire wall was adorned with smatterings of color—canvases showing fleets of swans against a cerulean sky, and sunflowers with tiny human shapes as its seeds. I eyed his movements while practicing my own recitation. Later, the room would fill with spectators eager for the exhibit showcasing the national River of Words winners; his brushstroke, my free verse poetry. Yet how would the audience take in the gilded wingtips of his swans, or interpret the stanzas I had written on the nexus of nature and memory? As young, budding artists, we held onto our creations with the same kind of muted hesitancy.

Over lunch and fragmented English, our initial connection began to crystallize. Here we were: Robhullah Hassani, Afghani schoolboy refugee living in Quetta, Pakistan, and this five-foot-tall Chinese girl with a weakness for Milton. Our extensive, gesture-dominated interaction revealed differences intertwined with similar backdrops. With his hand outlining a paintbrush's movement in the air, Robhullah explained his use of pastel mediums to sketch a country where beauty was relinquished for the harsher priorities of war. I spoke of the hours spent writing poetry about the Gobi plains and Connecticut shoreline. Our stories were about balance. For him, it meant the coexistence of beauty and destruction. For me, it meant choosing between the arid, tribal deserts of my childhood and the beaches of my present home, two cultural realities that often seem impossible to reconcile in words.

Yet I could not attain Robhullah's complete essence through conversation alone. I gained only fractions with the sharing of our chosen mediums which were, after all, abstractions to explain the inexplicable parts of reality. Much of our expanse was still left unexplored, solitary. When the car stopped, our vulnerabilities unmasked. We were about to face the waiting audience together. Between us, there was a profound necessity for unification and power.

We needed absolute sincerity. We needed a gesture of humanness. We needed simplicity. In that moment, we moved past the realm of the abstract. Past cultural undertones. Past the barriers of language and ethnocentric bias. Even past the shelters we built in art itself. This brought us to the simplest medium of all. As the car's engines quieted, I heard what the boy had been trying to tell me. "Take my hand." Robhullah was saying, his eyes soft around the edges. "Please, take my hand." We touched fingers. Distance fell away. The last fragment of solitude between us would tremble then dissipate. I may never forget his poignant plea, its resounding echo, and its outstretched hand.

Columbia Essay #2 (Common)

The author of this essay was admitted to Columbia University, Class of 2016.

I'm convinced that the most profound word is quantum. Add mechanics after it and you got a behemoth 90 years in the making. When I first heard it, I told myself, "I'm never going to know this". I mean imagine a science where every prediction you make should be counterintuitive. There, that's quantum mechanics.

At first, it was just something that physicists cared about. I was just a student trying to make the grade. Then a man named Dr. Quantum jumped into the picture. I was trying to understand how particles could be waves and waves could be particles, and when my textbook failed, I decided to check out YouTube. Five minutes later, a lot changed. "A lot" can be summed up in three words, "observer created reality". A few weeks later, the Quantum Enigma found its way into my hands and a year later, science literature replaced the science fiction as my favorite source of reading. Not that I felt sorry for Jules Verne or Isaac Asimov because Michio Kaku and Neil de Grasse Tyson still sound like science fiction authors when I delve into Physics of the Impossible or Death by Black Hole.

I hope I can still be a good scientist now that philosophy has gotten duct-taped into my scientific thoughts. From the humorous Schrödinger's Cat to Bell's mystical inequality, it looks like science has collided head on with the humanist question, why? Why am I here? Why is the universe the way it is? It's a powerful battle because I believe science is a justification for life as I see it. Everything that appeals to our fundamental nature, like free will, appears to be worth doing simply because the humans create reality through observation in the universe. When I held the classical worldview of clockwork, everything had a destiny. Aside from always waking up before the sun does and trudging to school like a zombie, I'm not sure it can. The world under quantum mechanics is purely random, except for me. Every moment of consciousness builds a piece of reality. Laughter, a smile, and a hug are all subtle forces that shape how I think and how I construct the world around me. If I'm happy, the world is bright. If I'm not, then the world is gray.

I liken quantum mechanics to The Matrix. You can talk about the matrix, but you really have to see it for yourself to know what it really is. Everything that I interpret in quantum mechanics, I'll never be able to prove with science (as it is now). Unfortunately, that's the nature of the beast and also why it's such a stubborn science. It has never produced a wrong prediction, yet scientists like my chemistry teacher tell me to disregard the implications and use it "for all practical purposes". Quantum refers to the smallest things in the universe but encompasses the biggest things in our consciousness. I long to know the true meaning of the word quantum and the worlds behind it.

The author of this essay was admitted to Columbia University, Class of 2019.

What single activity listed in the activity section of your Common Application are you most proud of and why? (150 words or less)

I am most proud of my work at George Mason University's GENRI Program. As an intern, I was able to apply all that I had learned in school in the real world with professors and graduate students. I was able to use my AP Computer Science knowledge to organize the World Meteorology Organization's (WMO) website. AP Statistics was useful in reading and writing scientific research papers. I did not think I would ever find the P-test or chi-squared test outside of my AP Statistics Classroom. Finally, I was able to use my communication and collaboration skills to help set up a joint research effort between George Mason and the U.S. Department of Agriculture (USDA). I am most proud of this research not only because I published a scientific paper, but also because I was able to use skills taught in school in the real world.

List the titles of the required readings from courses during the school year or summer that you enjoyed most in the past year. (150 words or less)

The Boy Who Harnessed the Wind by William Kamkwamba and Bryan Mealer

Outliers: The Story of Success by Malcolm Gladwell

The Geeks Shall Inherit the Earth by Alexandra Robbins

Frederick Douglass by Frederick Douglass

1984 by George Orwell

Principles of Economics by Greg Mankiw

Things Fall Apart by Chinua Achebe

Romeo and Juliet by Shakespeare

Othello by Shakespeare

Divergent by Veronica Roth (yes it was required)

The Odyssey (Poem by Homer)

A Tale of Two Cities by Charles Dickens

All Quiet on the Western Front by Erich Maria Remarque

List the titles of the books you read for pleasure that you enjoyed most in the past year. (150 words or less)

Freakonomics by Steven D. Levitt and Stephen J. Dubner

Naked Economics by Charles Wheelan

Immortal life of Henrietta lacks by Rebecca Skloot

The Disappearing Spoon by Sam Kean

Brave New World by Aldous Huxley

Animal Farm by George Orwell

The Lightning Thief and the Percy Jackson Series by Rick Riordan

Heroes of Olympus series by Rick Riordan

Ranger's Apprentice Series by John Flanagan

Eragon, The Eldest, Brisingr by Christopher Paolini

The Ender's Game by Orson Scott Card

Lord of the Flies by William Golding

List the titles of the print, electronic publications and websites you read regularly. (150 words or less)

American Chemical Society (ACS) publications (acs.org)

Politico.com

Wall Street Journal

The Onion (electronic publication)

New York Times

Washington Post

The Onion (electronic publication)

Reader's Digest

Science (magazine)

Reddit.com many subreddits including science, askreddit, MFA
http://www.iflscience.com

Yahoo News

Humans of New York

Didyouknowblog.com

List the titles of the films, concerts, shows, exhibits, lectures and other entertainments you enjoyed most in the past year. (150 words or less)

House of cards (TV Series)

Suits (TV Series)

Thesis on a homicide directed by Hernán Golfrd (international film)

Into the Silent Sea by Andrej Landin (international short film)

Colbert Report

National Public Radio (NPR), notably marketplace and "Wait Wait…Don't Tell Me!"

TED Talks notably "The Transformative power of classical music" by Benjamin Zander

"How I harnessed the wind" by William Kamkwamba, and "A 12-year Old App Developer" by Thomas Suarez

The Big Bang Theory (TV Series)

Phantom of the Opera on Broadway

Wicked on Broadway

The Social Network (movie)

Inception (movie)

Now You See Me (movie)

Please tell us what you find most appealing about Columbia and why? (300 words or less)

The summer of 2014, I visited Columbia wanting to know more about what Columbia could offer me. Up to this point, I had always known Columbia to excel at humanities from both talk with my counselor and my time at Columbia Model United Nations Conference and Exposition. Although I am heavily involved in debate and model United Nations, my time at Garcia MRSEC summer research program and George Mason University had piqued my interest in environmental science and material science. I knew little of Columbia's engineering so I had doubts whether Columbia would be right for me.

I felt a few drops of rain on my head as we approached an antique building during the campus tour. The tour guide boasted how Columbia had a great research program, mentioning that the first uranium atom had been split right across from where we were standing (and five levels below) in Pupin Hall. Due to the poor weather, the tour was suspended and we were forced inside. I took this opportunity to ask my tour guide about the research opportunities at Columbia. I was exhilarated to find out how easily Columbia students were able to do research. The tour guide told me of a friend of hers who just emailed a professor and now is doing a nine month research project in India.

Intrigued by the tour, I researched more about Columbia and found the Fu engineering school to be very fitting. I found everything I was interested in at Columbia Engineering: Environmental Science, Materials Science, a great model United Nations community, and on top of that finance and economics courses I would not be able to take at a traditional engineering school.

Looking back at Columbia from the metro entrance, I cast my doubts away. I had found a great fit.

For applicants to The Fu Foundation School of Engineering and Applied Science, please tell us what from your current and past experiences (either academic or personal) attracts you specifically to the field or fields of study that you noted in the Member Questions section. (300 words or less)

As I entered high school, I was bombarded with questions of what I wanted to be when I grew up. A Doctor? A Fireman? Perhaps a Lawyer? However at that point I had no idea what career I wanted to pursue much less what I wanted to major in college.

The summer of freshman year, I decided to apply to an internship at George Mason University. I was exhilarated to be able to work with graduate students and professors on climate research. I had access to data and research I would not have been able to get my hands on at my high school. I was so intrigued by the work I did that I decided to continue my work my sophomore summer. The second year, I actually got to travel to Washington D.C. to the U.S. Department of Agriculture (USDA) headquarters to discuss a potential collaboration between George Mason University and USDA.

Despite my success and joy at the GENRI program, I wished to explore other topics of science. The next summer, I had the pleasure of attending Garcia Materials and Science and Engineering Center's (MRSEC) Summer Program. There, I had the variety of engineering choices in front of me from dental pulp stem cells to fuel cells to even computational modeling. During the lectures where the professors tried to sell their topics, I became hooked to solar cells. These were not the everyday solar cells that you had lying around at home.

These solar cells were made entirely of organic material and were much cheaper than silicon solar cells. The research I conducted aimed to improve these organic solar cells to surpass their inorganic counterparts.

These two programs drastically influenced me on specifically what fields of study I wanted to pursue.

The author of this essay was admitted to Columbia University, Class of 2019.

Some students have a background or story that is so central to their identity that they believe their application would be incomplete without it. If this sounds like you, then please share your story.

The dark menacing clouds loomed above. Every week at this time, I would help serve lunch to the residents of the Katherine K. Hanley Family Shelter. Today, though, the sinister darkness in the sky, a harbinger of a snowstorm, frowned upon me. Although my parents were against it, I decided to drive to the shelter that stormy Saturday morning.

My days at the shelter were the same, an unchanging routine. As usual, I entered the kitchen, put on my earphones, and started to sweep. Soon, I had lost myself in the rhythm of my steady sweeping, of my familiar music. My isolation was broken only by the occasional resident passing by for coffee: a bright "hello," a few pleasant words, a final "thank you."

Suddenly, a tug on my shirt broke my concentration. Startled, I took off my earphones and turned to find a fourteen year old African American boy with a snapback and saggy jeans. "Could I help you out?" he asked. "Sure," I responded tentatively.

The first minutes went by silently except for the swishing of the brooms. "What's your name?" I asked, trying to break the ice.

"Joshua", he responded, "although most of my friends just call me Josh."

From that moment on, we hit it off. We talked about anything that came to mind. He too was a basketball fan, and we talked about the upcoming March Madness tournament and our favorite teams. I discovered how his mom was a single parent supporting four kids. "Thank God we got into this shelter, 'cause without it we would have nowhere to stay," he informed me. I asked where his siblings went to school. "Right now they go to Woodson, but you never know these days since we're moving so much."

I knew how hard moving could be. After moving to Virginia in fifth grade, I began to keep to myself, afraid of reaching out to others in this unfamiliar place. But now, listening to Josh, I couldn't imagine being in his place: not only moving time after time, but sometimes not even knowing where his family would stay.

Once it was time to serve food, Josh stayed by my side. He introduced me to some of the residents who I had never talked to, beyond pleasantries exchanged in the hallway. "That's Josiah, my second oldest brother" he pointed out, his brown eyes sparkling with pride. "He's really good at basketball!" I met Lisa, who lived in New York before she moved to Virginia in search of a job to support her child.

I discovered a newfound admiration for Josh. Despite having to move every few years, he still was able to make friends wherever he went, having the courage to approach new people and start simple yet meaningful conversations.

At 3 o'clock, when I was usually due back home, I looked outside only to find the roads paved white by a flurry of snow. I was stuck at the shelter. But talking to the residents and hearing their different backgrounds and individual stories, I barely felt the time passing. All these weeks, I had no idea I had been serving food to such diverse and intriguing people.

Though my conversation that day with Josh was simple, it truly was a turning point for me. I found the courage to break out of my normal routine and open up, learning how meaningful the simple act of getting to know someone could be.

Josh eventually found a home and moved out of the shelter. Despite his absence, I have continued to strike up conversations with those around me. Overcoming my routine, habits, and uncertainties, I have befriended people I never would have imagined befriending: residents, neighbors, teachers, strangers. By volunteering at the shelter, I had hoped to help my community. But thanks to my conversation with Josh, my time there also taught me to become more connected to it.

Sharlene was admitted to Columbia University, Class of 2019.

Please tell us what you find most appealing about Columbia and why? (300 words or less)

The variety of ways Columbia promotes and fosters intellectual stimulation is unparalleled. At first glance, the Core Curriculum's focus on humanities would clash with my interest in science and engineering, but in reality, immersing myself in the liberal arts would bolster my endeavors in the technical field. For instance, the University Writing class would improve my skills as a writer because as an engineer, I must clearly convey my ideas. Furthermore, seminars about culture and ethics would be crucial to better understanding the controversy surrounding drone technology. If I wish to further develop unmanned air systems, a Columbia education would ensure I have the critical thinking skills to address and resolve such concerns.

In addition to the strong academic program, the opportunities outside the classroom would allow both my creativity and innovation to thrive. The student-run publications would be ideal for channeling my love of writing, science, and humor. One day, I could gush about Google's wifi drones for the Columbia Science Review, and the next day, I could publish a satirical rant about New York traffic for The Fed. On the technical side, the recently opened Columbia Maker Space would be essential to an aspiring engineer. I often visit my local makerspace to 3D print models I've created on SolidWorks, so I'm thankful a similar facility is available where I could produce prototypes to test my designs.

A course on mechanical systems is not an obstacle I would overcome for a piece of paper at graduation; it is a tool I would use to improve drone technology. Columbia University provides its students with a plethora of opportunities for cultivating critical thinking inside and outside the classroom, and by taking full advantage of the resources offered, I will one day realize my dream of working with unmanned air systems.

CHAPTER 3
Cornell University Application Essay

Cornell University

Ithaca, New York

2015 admission results: 6,234 offers out of 41,907 applicants, 14.9%

2014 admission rate: 14.0%

Justin was admitted to Cornell University, Class of 2019.

Describe two or three of your current intellectual interests and why they are exciting to you. Why will Cornell's College of Arts and Sciences be the right environment in which to pursue your interests? (Please limit your response to 650 words.)

My research at the Diabetes Research Program at NYU Medical Center has piqued my interest in biological research. Having spent a few months at the lab under the supervision of a postdoctorate fellow, I have become acquainted with and came to truly admire the level of dedication researchers have to their work. My postdoc mentor helped me realize that it is this dedication, this toiling of researchers in labs, that helps promote and advance the field, especially one as enigmatic as medicine. I want to continue to engage myself in lab work, to immerse myself in the forefront of scientific studies. The constant excitement that comes from trying to connect one piece of the puzzle with another keeps me continually engrossed in my work. Cornell's College of Arts and Sciences is the right environment to pursue my interests in biological research because so many options are available to undergraduates. The resources at my disposal allow me to get my hands dirty, and really involve myself in the work, something I couldn't always do as a high school student. The talented faculty and mentors that work at the plethora of cutting edge facilities covering a vast array of disciplines in the College of Arts and Sciences creates an attractive environment to continue the spirit of exploration that epitomizes research.

One thing I find appealing about philosophy is that they can come in many forms and from many sources. In the shallow breadth of books I have encountered in English class alone, I was confronted with not a small number of inputs regarding our existence, what constitutes reality, and the nature of knowledge. It is as if every author, from the well known Voltaire to the obscure science fiction writer Le Guin, has light to shed on the philosophical questions that pervade mankind since before history. Philosophy continues to be an interest of mine because these fundamental problems have overarching implications that affect how we see ourselves as people, thinkers, or individuals in society. Studying philosophy is much like studying ourselves, and by learning from the greats and their thoughts, I can come to realize my own thoughts and what I see myself as. The College of Arts and Sciences' philosophy department offers numerous courses at various levels, so that a beginner like myself has somewhere to start, as well as a general direction to work towards. The small classes and idiosyncrasies in our upbringings as future Cornell students are sure to contribute to eye opening discussions.

CHAPTER 4
Dartmouth College Application Essay

Dartmouth College

Hanover, New Hampshire

2015 admission results: 2,120 offers out of 20,504 applicants, 10.3%

2014 admission rate: 11.5%

Dartmouth Essay (Common)

The author of this essay was admitted to Dartmouth College, Class of 2018.

On the first day of school three years ago, our teaching assistant finished gathering everyone's homework and realized there was one without a name on it. He walked around the classroom, asking the girls if it was theirs, skipping me several times during the check. I suddenly realized that I had forgotten to write my name and told him. For a few seconds he looked at me skeptically, not believing that the big guy in front of him, recently recruited to the school's basketball team, could have such neat handwriting. I have actually had nice handwriting since elementary school, when I was tutored in calligraphy every week and also took a handwriting class offered by my school. Most people don't expect me to have good handwriting, and similar scenes have happened several times. In fact, it's not the only time I have defied the expectations of those around me.

My friends are always shocked to learn that I am interested in many things they consider "feminine". I have all kinds of medical products in my dorm room and always help my teammates treat their wounds after practice and games. I always sew torn buttons back onto my shirts and keep my clothing both clean and ironed. I have long been interested in gardening and am extremely careful while planting flowers. I love to plant tulips because of their bright colors and cup-like shape, as well as the Sago Palm plant, which I learned how to take care of from my grandfather when I was young.

I first developed these seemingly contradictory traits when I was younger and my mother tried hard to make me adopt "good" habits. The most common of these was asking me to collect the toys from my floor. At first, I was resistant, like most other boys of my age. However, one day I became tired of my messy room and her constant reminders, and cleaned up after myself. I found great benefit from doing so and always kept my things organized after that. I have many other traits that seem to be contradictory. For example, I enjoy many abstract forms of learning like art and music. I learned traditional painting when I was young, and enjoy going to symphony concerts, as well as visiting art museums. But I can also do more "crude" tasks, like repair motors and other mechanical parts. I once helped my friend's dad repair his car engine and built a remote control helicopter with an uncle.

Even my mindset tries to juggle different perspectives. For instance, I am both prudent and confident. When deciding whether to study in America, I spent many nights researching and listing the advantages and disadvantages of studying abroad. Finally, after talking with many people and hesitating for a long time, I made up my mind and signed my name on the form, eager for a new adventure. Once I made the decision, I removed all doubt from my mind and looked forward to my move.

I don't regard these contradictory traits as a burden. Being contradictory can be very practical. Having a wide range of interests has given me a diverse group of friends, exposed me to many different activities, and helped me handle difficult decisions with varied perspectives. Sticking to the role society assigned would leave me stuck behind artificial barriers and limit my options, just like how men often push away what is considered "feminine". But I have found that it quite enriching to take the best from both sides. There are many doors that can be unlocked. Being contradictory lets me have my unique perspective and an open attitude towards many things, allowing me to explore all aspects of life.

CHAPTER 5
Duke University Application Essays

Duke University

Durham, North Carolina

2015 admission results: 3,534 offers out of 31,150 applicants, 11.3%

2014 admission rate: 10.8%

Skye was admitted to Duke University, Class of 2019.

Picture this: A Chinese woman sits in Molecular Genetics class at SUNY Stony Brook. She realizes she forgot her pens. In her limited English, she turns around to the nerdy boy in glasses in the seat next to her, and asks to borrow one of his. Later, she asks for his notes. Even later, he asks her to dinner. Thus, a love story was born. Three years after, as a result of one fateful day in Molecular Genetics and the combined molecular genetics of my mother and father, I was born.

Sometimes, I think about how my parents could have easily gone through life without meeting each other. I think about the minute details, the little things, that could have prevented my existence, and I am overwhelmed. The combination of these arbitrary coincidences that brought my parents together from opposite sides of the world is unfathomable. There have been infinite moments before me; there will be infinite moments after. As such, the moments in which I am here, those moments, those are the ones that matter.

Recently, I read Slaughterhouse Five by Kurt Vonnegut, a novel that deals with the slippery concept of time. One scene in particular struck a deep chord with me. The narrator is pondering his life, and he thinks: "And I asked myself about the present: how wide it was, how deep it was, how much was mine to keep". Time is relative, as theorized by Einstein. Time is a human construct, a limited resource, a key ingredient in why I am here. My parent's timing was impeccable.

The moments that are the present quickly become the past, and the future that looms ahead turns slowly into the present. At present, I am here, typing this essay, trying to compile my seventeen years of past into one comprehensive picture. I remember why I am here. I remember what I have done, what I have learned, and I try to discern how to put this into words for someone to read in the future. I am here to do something, to discover who I am, to maybe even try and understand why humans are here. Why do we ask why? I am here to use this mass of tissue inside my skull to create something, an idea, a discovery, an accident (hopefully a fortuitous one, like penicillin, or plastic). I am here to understand the plight of humans, to empathize, to educate, to learn. I am here to create music, to create memories. Memories have been created.

I am here, on the third planet from the sun, in the year 2014 C.E. asking myself why I am here and not somewhere else. I am here because the Earth is the perfect temperature to sustain life. But then I think about the delicate balance of nature, and global warming, and maybe I am here to find a solution. I am here to investigate possibilities. I have studied the effect of climate change; I want to know more. I want to prevent it so more people can be here in the future. I have worked in a lab with scientists who are trying to uncover the key to cancer cell metastasis. I am here to uncover the secrets of the cell, because these secrets are key to understanding the bigger picture. They are key to understanding afflictions like pain, genetic disease, Alzheimers. I am here as a scientist and not someone else, because science combats ignorance. I am here as a musician, as a flute player, as one member of a band whose individual artistic expression blends to form a cohesive, beautiful sound. I am here as a soloist, to interpret the music personally, to tell a story, to convey emotion. I am here as a marcher, to reach my dot and not someone else's, to work as a cog in the machine that is our Stranded show or our Chicago show, a show that no other band has or will ever perform. I am here as an artist, to share my experiences so that others can understand me.

All I know for certain is that I am fortunate to be here, in a time where women can be educated and I can have parents of different races. I am fortunate that my parents met, that I have the opportunities my grandparents did not, that I can read and write and play flute and march and learn science. I am one of 7 billion who are here on Earth, one of 316.1 million who are here in the United States, and one of 9 million here in North Carolina. Although there is much to be fixed in our society, I am glad I am here and not somewhere else. My mother was somewhere else, and she came here, to the United States, in order to find opportunity. I am here because of her sacrifice, her dedication, and her triumph against all odds. I am uncertain of my destination, but at present, I hope it will be the Duke University.

Duke Essay #2 (Common)

Skye was admitted to Duke University, Class of 2019.

One thing all students should know before high school graduation: Find a community that helps you thrive. For me, that community was marching band. I joined marching band in the summer of 2011. Originally, I was unsure if I wanted to do marching band or try out for tennis; however, I quickly realized I made the right decision. Tennis is a sport for the individual, while marching band can only succeed with cohesive cooperation along with individual determination. Marching band has allowed me to be part of a community of dedicated and creative students and has changed my life in immeasurable ways.

Marching band is beautiful because about eighty students work and sweat and persevere together to produce an end product that conveys a story in such a complex and unique manner. It is physically and emotionally demanding. Nevertheless, we all enjoy every practice because we know the end product will demonstrate the effort we exerted. Being a leader in marching band has taught me how to effectively balance the role of friend and mentor. It has made me strive to be on my best behavior at all times because I know others are looking to me for guidance as a role model. I have led the flute section for the past two years. We have become extremely close, and at times practices can start to deteriorate into silliness when one flautist decides to hip-bump an unwary friend (a tradition that somehow developed in our section). As a leader, it is my responsibility to make sure everyone stays attentive and respectful. My section knows that when I say "go to set", it's time to focus.

I have made my best friends through the band. Band is like a second family. Not only do we care about the show that we put on the field, but every member cares about their fellow band mates. Recently, our band suffered a tragedy when a recent graduate passed away unexpectedly. He was a cherished friend, and our band held a beautiful memorial service on the field. Everyone provided support and shared memories. Although many were grieving, having our band family helped us overcome the loss. I know that not every sports team or club is as tightly knit as the Chapel Hill High marching band, so I am grateful to have been able to participate in such a welcoming and caring community.

Marching band has shown me the meaning of dedication, focus, and discipline. Although many believe that band members merely walk around the field while playing their instrument, the reality is completely different. The hard work is always worthwhile. Many of my best memories from high school are band related, like the late night bus rides after competitions when we sing our show at the top of our lungs, or running in the rain at band camp, or the freezing cold holiday parade mornings. Marching band has meant so much to me, and I hope I can continue with marching band in college.

CHAPTER 6
Harvard University Application Essay

Harvard University

Cambridge, Massachusetts

2015 admission results: 2,081 offers out of 37,307 applicants, 5.6%

2014 admission rate: 5.9%

Emily was admitted to Harvard University, Class of 2018.

You may wish to include an additional essay if you feel the college application forms do not provide sufficient opportunity to convey important information about yourself or your accomplishments. You may write on a topic of your choice, or you may choose from one of the following topics:

- *Unusual circumstance in your life*
- *Travel or living experiences in other countries*
- *A list of books you have read during the past twelve months*
- *How you hope to use your college education*
- *An intellectual experience (course, project, book, discussion, paper, poetry, or research topic in engineering, mathematics, science, or other modes of inquiry) that has meant the most to you*
- *What you would want your future college roommate to know about you*

Katie and Lindsay were in a serious fight. They were both looking for my opinion on whose fault it was for ditching the sleepover, and my indecisive sixth grade self was scrambling for a peaceful resolution. This was the first time I had to decide whether to sacrifice part of my own opinion on an issue (clearly Katie totally blew off Taylor when she went to hang out with her more popular friends) and come up with a compromise that made everyone happy.

As I've grown older, I have somehow become a magnet for mediating conflicts among friends. People consider me trustworthy enough to know their deepest troubles and worries, but rational enough to find a solution to these problems. In fact, the awkward neutral zone between two fighting friends has been a constant, stressful place.

It was my friend Sarah who first compared me to Stella. We were at my house, laughing about how I had a critical essay due the next day even though I hadn't started reading A Streetcar Named Desire when she grabbed my wrists mid-laugh, insisting I was identical to Stella, and not just because I was born in

Louisiana. I scoffed and told her that didn't make any sense. I didn't have a crazy sister, and I most definitely would not have been stupid enough to marry a tyrannical drunk. However, after I finally started reading the play, I realized I did have much in common with Stella Kowalski.

During arguments, she straddles the fence in her defense of her sister and husband depending on whom she is speaking to. By allowing both sides to see where the other is coming from, Stella resolves multiple confrontations. I have taken up this method to address problems on a downplayed high school standard, where petty issues escalate to dramatic levels.

Last swim season, Taylor, an underclassman, lashed out at the "mean, hateful" coach for telling her to lose weight, while the coach, exasperated by Megan's increasing sensitivity, only wanted to give advice to his swimmer but had no idea how to phrase it. By trying to talk out the situation with both the coach and Megan, and by simply saying that no, the coach is not trying to destroy Taylor's swimming career, or that yes, Taylor actually genuinely cared about her performance, I tried to get both sides to acknowledge the opposite opinion. Instead of agreeing wholeheartedly with either of them, I try to help them see the reason that their anger blocked and to point out that their frustration does not have to be so severe.

When Stella does have to pick a side, her reasoning does not come from any strong opinions against Blanche, or for Stanley, but rather from the environment she is left in. She chooses the easiest way to solve the problem. If reasoning with both sides doesn't work, I either make sure the argument reaches a conclusion or I choose the side that corresponds with my own morals. For instance, in my household, I have learned it is always better to take my sister's side.

Several years ago I told my mom that my sister had been watching Hannah Montana instead of practicing violin. For a week, she was insulted by every one of my actions and transformed from a sweet, caring girl to a monster that pounced on all my mistakes. She had no more qualms about siding with my parents against me on everything. Without the coalition between sisters to rely on, the household quickly fell into a disarray of alliances and resentments. My little sister needs my loyalty and support more than my parents do, and since then, I have been careful in choosing a side during an argument.

After Sarah's offhand comparison, I began to realize that my methods as a mediator were not unique. Stella's priorities aren't portrayed in how much she yells or rants or lashes out, but through her ultimate decision and the way she resolves the problems between Blanche and Stanley. Because of Stella's similar experiences, I have realized that my role of being "stuck in the middle" is actually important.

CHAPTER 7

Johns Hopkins University Application Essay

Johns Hopkins University

Baltimore, Maryland

2015 admission results: 3,065 offers out of 24,717 applicants, 14.2%

2014 admission rate: 12.8%

The author of this essay was admitted to Johns Hopkins University, Class of 2018.

Biting back a cry of pain, my mother came stumbling down the stairs. I had just arrived home to find her in a hospital gown, barely awake and holding her side. She had not come home the night before, but my father had made up a bizarre excuse for her absence and I did not question it.

However, instead of coming home to a mother who had been stranded in New York, I found one who had spent the night in the hospital after having her lymph nodes removed for cancer screening. After hearing about the surgery, I locked my door and cried until my throat burned and my eyes were too swollen to see. My mother, my one and only mother, might be at death's door.

Her treatment was six months of poison. I watched her hair fall out in little chunks all over the house until we had to shave her head as tears poured down her face. Despite the crying, my mother's strength stunned me; I never saw her vomit, though I knew the drugs nauseated her. She motivated me to find power I did not know I possessed at age thirteen. For the first time in my life, I completed chores, helped my sister with schoolwork, and spent as much time talking to my mother as I could. I did everything in my ability to make her more comfortable while somehow managing to live through the legendary first day of high school.

Throughout that time, I transformed from the girl everyone could hear a mile down the hall to one who just stepped back and listened to conversations. My mind roamed through the "big questions" in life as each day, I did not know if I would come home to a mother who would live twenty more years, or one. Though some may call my change a bout of depression, it allowed my world to expand beyond the material worries of a slightly spoiled child as I encountered the awe-provoking miracles and heart-wrenching anguish life can provide. Seeing both ends of the spectrum gave me a new perspective, inspiring me to work harder for my dreams while still remembering to appreciate all that I have.

The growing process was not easy. At times, I felt completely powerless against this all-consuming disease. I continuously researched my mother's cancer in hopes of miraculously discovering "the cure", but what I found was far from encouraging. The only remedies seemed as poisoning as the illness itself. I am determined to see Cancer's downfall. I will dedicate everything I have to lessen its physical and psychological wounds, both in a laboratory and with patients because sometimes, a little hope is worth as much as a new drug. My mother's reminders that the road to this career is long and challenging have strengthened my resolve as I continue down the path, for her, and for everyone who has suffered like her, or like me.

Three years later, my mother is still winning her battle and I seek to ensure others do as well.

CHAPTER 8
Massachusetts Institute of Technology Application Essays

Massachusetts Institute of Technology

Cambridge, Massachusetts

2015 admission results: 1,467 offers out of 18,306 applicants, 8.0%

2014 admission rate: 7.7%

MIT Essay #1

Sharlene was admitted to Massachusetts Institute of Technology, Class of 2019.

We know you lead a busy life, full of activities, many of which are required of you. Tell us about something you do for the pleasure of it. (100 words or fewer)

There are worlds in my head. By writing science fiction, I share their histories and cultures. My heroes sleep with night lights, and my villains bake cakes between imperial conquests. While I do have a blast fleshing out quirky characters, I invest most of my passion in creating universes that answer my "What if?" questions. Science fiction allows me to explore how memory transfer can shape society, what results when the laws of physics are rewritten, and so forth. I want to give the impossible a chance to exist, and writing is how I bring my imagination to life.

Although you may not yet know what you want to major in, which department or program at MIT appeals to you and why? (100 words or fewer)

I'm drawn towards mechanical engineering, especially the Design, Manufacturing, and Product Development courses. I use CAD software to illustrate the models I imagine, and with 3D printers, my ideas become tangible. By incorporating my obsession with 3D printing into engineering, I hope to apply new knowledge of mechanical systems to make additive manufacturing more efficient. I satisfy my mind by designing gear systems and cute trinkets, while my hands are itching to test the effectiveness of 3D printers with multiple nozzles or cylindrical frames. With an education in mechanical engineering, I can improve the technology that helped my creativity thrive.

What attribute of your personality are you most proud of, and how has it impacted your life so far? This could be your creativity, effective leadership, sense of humor, integrity, or anything else you'd like to tell us about. (200-250 words)

Humor has always been my favorite mode of communication. The witty comments inserted into my chemistry lecture notes elicited positive reactions from the grader, and the exchange of clever banter between me and my calculus teacher became an integral part of the class. (I'd throw in a physics pun if it didn't sound so forced.)

In all seriousness, I can't be serious. As a child, whenever my sibling became upset, my first instinct used to be to dramatize my actions and make them laugh. Not only did it brighten their moods, but they also forgot I was the one who originally made them cry. I write satire for the school paper because I best convey my opinions when they're slathered thick with irony. Writing angry or solemn pieces just isn't my style. After noticing severe dress code violations at school, I published a rant about girls revealing too much ankle and guys neglecting to bring their top hats and bejeweled walking sticks.

I've discovered that building rapport with people is also much easier after testing the waters with a joke or two. Without much knowledge of the other person's interests, I can still grow closer to them by making them laugh. Not every moment is a laughing matter, but I know when to apply humor to liven a situation. The more comfortable I feel about acting goofy in public, the more confident I become as well, because my sense of humor plays a pivotal role in my self-expression.

Benjamin was admitted to Massachusetts Institute of Technology, Class of 2019.

We know you lead a busy life, full of activities, many of which are required of you. Tell us about something you do for the pleasure of it. (100 Words)

Whenever I practice parkour, I feel the cool air flowing past me. I see the obstacles I leave in my wake. Railings don't slow me down and walls can't stop my progress. The usual flow of life becomes a vibrant explosion of activity and freedom. Although parkour is classically defined as a way of moving through one's environment as efficiently as possible, I feel it is also a way of expressing myself in an unprecedented way. Parkour frees me from the boundaries and barriers we place on ourselves and provide the creativity to treat everywhere like a modern playground.

What attribute of your personality are you most proud of, and how has it impacted your life so far? This could be your creativity, effective leadership, sense of humor, integrity, or anything else you'd like to tell us about. (200-250 words)

If you ask my friends about me, and my personality, their first adjectives would be caring, funny, silly, and laid-back, but never smart. "Smart" would be one of those adjectives that describe me well, but only after a moment of reflection. Many people may think that's a bad thing, but I say exactly the opposite.

I'm pleased to be described as funny or laid-back by my friends, because they display the balance in my life. No, not just keeping my two feet on the ground, but the metaphorical balance between work and play. In the classroom, I can be calm, focused and intellectual, but once that's done for the day, it's time to relax. I pride myself on being the approachable, energetic guy with a sense of humor, the one in the heat of a conversation with friends.

Even when there's balance, however, doesn't mean that there has to be a strict divider between the two. Sure, physics problems are no joke, but that doesn't stop my humor from showing when the textbook decides to have Jill run at 90% the speed of light. Just because I think clearly in the classroom doesn't mean I can't outside of it. In fact, many of my extracurricular activities require the traits I have in the classroom: strategy games, trading card games, word puzzles, music, you name it.

These traits inside and outside the classroom come together nicely to create a unique, balanced blend of human that I'm proud to be.

- Approachable
- Self confidence
- Humorous, relaxed, mix of fun and concentration
- Clarity of thought (teaching and such)
- Curiosity
- Helpfulness
- Play off parkour essay (that showed freedom and energy and focused) and physics (calm)
- Work/play balance and intermingling. Creates life balance by making each facet better

Tell us about the most significant challenge you've faced or something important that didn't go according to plan. How did you manage the situation? (200-250 words)

After my first robotics season, I wished I had joined earlier. We built all sorts of robots from a cubic foot in size to a cubic meter. I had enjoyed myself throughout the build season, yet something didn't seem quite right. In fact, many members were not at all satisfied with the club. There was a fundamental unfairness in the way opportunities were distributed.

Only a few students got assigned to the big robots, while everyone else got delegated to a smaller project. Even though I was one of the lucky few to work on the big robot, I immediately felt bad for the neglected students and began pushing for a club-wide restructuring in both leadership and overall logistics.

Eventually, the movement gained momentum and we began to make a mark on the club structure. As we became a student-run club rather than a parent-run organization, more students became involved in running the club. The parents passed down the metaphorical torch, and we became the new club leaders. However, now that we did have the power to resolve the problems, we couldn't agree on the correct combination of changes to keep everyone happy.

In the end, we decided to split the club into several sections that specialized in one aspect of the robot. With a rotation system in place, we were able to get the "veterans" to not keep to themselves and instead mentor others and let everyone get a chance at contributing to the big robot.

Although you may not yet know what you want to major in, which department or program at MIT appeals to you and why? (100 Words)

Ever since I first took physics, I've felt attracted to its complex problems, yet simple underlying concepts. My mom decided to get me a book titled "For the Love of Physics". Reading this book, I immediately slipped into a feeling of calm and content: I had found my place among the physicists. The charismatic Dr. Lewin walked me through the feelings of wonder and excitement in physics that very much resonated with who I was. Every time I hear news of MIT discoveries, I feel like the MIT Physics community is the one I want to be part of.

Describe the world you come from; for example, your family, clubs, school, community, city, or town. How has that world shaped your dreams and aspirations? (200-250 words)

- Physics teacher

Even though I didn't go to the Thomas Jefferson High School for Science and Technology, it turns out that Oakton was actually the perfect environment that nurtured my intellectuality and allowed me to use initiative take control of my education through academic freedom.

I discovered my love for physics when I took an AP Physics class as the only sophomore. At first I felt scared and alone, with no friends to band together with for the rough journey that laid ahead. However, Dr. Roudebush took an interest in me: She encouraged me to be engaged, and pushed me to achieve greater things. In addition to the class material, she instilled in us a deeper, more extensive reasoning behind the physics, and taught how numbers can truly be beautiful. In that class, I found a place to channel my ever-present curiosity and passion.

Senior year will be my third year with my physics teacher; we will begin quantum mechanics, relativity, and study for the Physics Olympiad. During last year's Physics Olympiad, I realized that although I was the only one to compete in the final round at my school, there are whole communities of physics-loving students who love the elegance of physics as much as I do. I look forward to joining one of these communities at MIT.

Benjamin was admitted to Massachusetts Institute of Technology, Class of 2019.

Describe a place or environment where you are perfectly content. What do you do or experience there, and why is it meaningful to you?

It seems redundant to say that physics is the world to me, since it literally is, yet that's exactly how I feel. Physics is the lens through which I experience the world. It's everywhere: from an elevator ride, to the acoustics of a movie theater, to sitting in a living room and admiring the grandfather clock, I am reminded of the ubiquity of physics. Even at basketball games, I see things differently: basketball player's legs, coiled up like a spring to counteract gravity and send him flying into the air, his joints and muscles providing the necessary torque to launch the ball and finally, the ball going through that perfect parabola into the hoop. Where some may see a fluid shooting motion, I see separate little physics movements working together towards a common goal and marvel at the shot nonetheless.

The excitement that comes from a basketball game can't compare to the feeling I get from sitting in that cool, silent classroom, pondering the newest Physics problem. The textbook makes the problems fun for us by breaking away from dry exercises in a silly, geeky way: "Suppose the coefficient of static friction for Swiss cheese and wood is." But personally, physics has always instilled a passion in me without having to calculate whether a block of cheese will topple over or slide off. The simple joy of figuring out the solution to real world problems such as the flight of an arrow or the levitating power of a magnet through pure mathematics is enough to keep me going on my adventure through the world of physics.

Through my exploration of physics, mysteries of the world that haunted me through childhood were revealed to me. Why are solar systems and galaxies so flat? Why IS the sky blue? These childhood mysteries of mine, born through an innate curiosity of the world, were finally solved though my exploration of physics; I learned about gravity's relationship with orbits, and about how molecules in the air scatter light.

However, this isn't the end of my journey. There are so many more questions in the world still left unanswered: What exactly is dark matter? What happens to mass as it enters a black hole? What is the future of our universe? Such questions ignite my inquisitiveness. I long to join the ranks of scientists: those who thirst for the undiscovered knowledge at our fingertips. If I was happy from solving a simple mechanics problem, one could only imagine my joy at discovering something new or creating knowledge for all of humanity.

I, for one, haven't lost my childhood curiosity. I take pride and comfort in discovering new things, in learning more about the world. My tool of choice on this grand adventure? Physics. Through physics I can learn about the inner workings of the world around us, following in the footsteps of the great scientists before our time such as Isaac Newton, the inventor of calculus, or James Clark Maxwell, who combined electricity and magnetism.

Through physics classes, I have walked these very same paths of discovery that physicists throughout past ages uncovered. Doing the same labs as these giants of physics made me realize how similar their drive for knowledge is to mine and pushed me to steadfastly pursue the same level of achievement and discovery in my studies. I hope to continue on my path of continual discovery and enlightenment throughout my college and professional career by expanding my knowledge and affection for my wonderful world of physics.

The author of this essay was admitted to Massachusetts Institute of Technology, Class of 2019.

Describe a place or environment where you are perfectly content. What do you do or experience there and why is it meaningful to you?

I stare down at the digits, neatly handwritten on a piece of scrap paper. It's a typical Tuesday night, and I sit cross-legged on the only open space on the floor of my dad's cramped office. But I never felt more comfortable. The daily struggles of a kindergartener find their corner in the back of my mind as I anxiously glance down at the paper on the floor. 1124 + 837. I follow the procedure as meticulously as I was taught. It's 1961. I jot down my answer under the line, aligning each digit properly. A grin forms form ear to ear as I proudly pass the paper to my dad, waiting for approval.

I still find myself as comfortable with numbers as I did in my dad's office. Yet, it is a new sense of contentment. It's not that I do not find myself elated calculating derivatives in calculus, but the arbitrary numbers I found comfort in began to take on meaning as I aged.

"Mark number 11!" You can call me 11, or 19, or 6. They are only three of my myriad aliases, but all represent the same part of me. For me, 11 is astroturf and noisome soccer cleats. It is blending into the machine – like functioning of a team, yet performing my individual role. It is exhilaration when the ball slips past the fingertips of the opposing team's goalie. It is the life-long friendships I am a quintessential part of.

You can also call me 5615, or 3887, or 1221. 5615 is calloused skin and fiberglass poles. It is hours spent sprinting down a narrow runway to launch myself over a bar. It is disappointment in breaking a pole in half, only to find it snapped because of a finally corrected technique. It is adrenaline pulsing through every inch of my body, achieving a personal record on the third and last attempt. It is every child's dream, defying gravity, soaring through the air.

Or just call me 37. 37 is a three hour bus ride at 4:00 in the morning. It is weeks of studying the differences between immunoglobulins A, D, E, G, and M and the layers of the dermis. It is the irreversible bonds and unforgettable memories formed between teammates. It is accomplishment when the only sound is the roar of applause walking up to the stage to receive a medal in a Science Olympiad competition.

I am content with adding because it forms my identity. I find myself in numbers. All I can wonder is what comes after 5615?

MIT Essay #5

The author of this essay was admitted to Massachusetts Institute of Technology, Class of 2019.

We know you lead a busy life, full of activities, many of which are required of you. Tell us something you do for the pleasure of it (less than 100 words).

Within a split second I found myself sprawled on the mat, grasping onto half of the pole, staring at the other half remaining in the pit.

It was nearing the end of the third hour of practicing my plant. It was so blissfully simple, but so impossibly difficult. I took one last run.

"You did it right!" he praised. "That's why it snapped!"

And that is the funny thing about pole vault: something has to break before it is right. Whether it is a mental wall or a pole, improvement cannot be made without something breaking. And I still have a lot of poles to break.

Although you may not yet know what you want to major in, which department or program at MIT appeals to you and why? (less than 100 words)

I often quizzically stare at the same poster in my friend's room; it reads "we see things not as they are but as we are." And I have to disagree. We see things exactly as they are.

Before this summer, I saw a caliper as simply a caliper, as anybody else would. But I spent the summer transforming a simple plastic caliper into a device to measure blood oxygenation levels in tumors.

Engineering intrigues me because it requires sight and insight: sight to see an object and insight to transform it. And it only requires engineering to turn vision into reality.

What attribute of your personality are you most proud of, and how has it impacted your life so far? This could be your creativity, effective leadership, sense of humor, integrity, or anything you'd like to tell us about (200-250 words).

"Hey dirtbag" I shouted to my friend as I watched a smile form on her face.

The two of us had recently become closer than ever in lieu of our circumstances. Both of us found companionship in each other, for we were both benched while we watched our five other senior friends play soccer.

The word dirtbag was an "inside joke" between us. It was the term her doctor used to describe the brain tumor in her head. She had explained to me what her doctor had explained to her. The tumor was the "dirtbag" in the classroom of smart kids, throwing spit balls and paper airplanes at the rest of the class. Once the dirtbag was removed, the rest of the class, or her brain, would be smarter. When she told me this, I did the only thing I could think of doing; I turned the analogy into a joke. We began to use the word quite often, cracking up at its mention.

As tough as my friend's life became, she never failed to make me laugh. Any moments spent together were full of laughter. We sat on the sidelines making what would have been miserable some of the best moments of my life.

My best accomplishments became the moments I put a smile on her face. As I sat in the hospital with her after she had been there for a week, I did as she had done for me for years. I returned the gift of laughter.

Describe the world you come from; for example, your family, clubs, school, community, city, or town. How has that world shaped your dreams and aspirations? (200-250 words)

Sometimes I feel as if I am starring in Snow White as one of the seven dwarfs. It's a bit different though; we are not in a fairytale, nor are we dwarfs. And we share a bond not created by mining and living together in the forest of talking animals, but by a coincidental shared love of soccer. Yet I always find myself accompanied by my own set of "dwarfs." They have different names too: Caring,

Creative, Awkward, Giddy, Smart, and Funny. And they have all taught me more than I could have ever learned about myself.

It is one of those rare nights that all of us are available to hang out together, one of those nights I wish could last forever. After ordering pizza and indulging in ice cream, Caring cleans up the table without a word of complaint. Creative is sitting at the piano, playing songs she memorized while Giddy sings along. Awkward is talking to Smart about her pronunciation of milk as "melk", both of them cracking up. And I'm sitting with Funny, doubled over in laughter.

Call me selfish, but I take a little part of each of them for myself. I give compassion to my friends just as Caring shows compassion for us. I find moments to laugh at myself, just as Awkward does, and look at situations with the light-heartedness of Giddy. I express Creative's free spirit through my artwork and Smart's intelligence in school. And I put smiles on people's faces with Funny's humor.

I don't know what name they would give me, but for now, you can just call me Sarah.

Tell us about the most significant challenge you've faces or something important that didn't go according to plan. How did you manage the situation? (200-250 words)

Snap. Crackle. Pop.

That is not the sound of your favorite breakfast cereal, but my knee when I tore my ACL.

"After surgery, you won't be able to resume physical activities for six months to a year" the surgeon stated quite bluntly. Those words seemed like a death sentence to me. I could not fathom not playing sports for up to a year. Yet I had to; it was my reality. As a soccer player, I witnessed people tear their ACL's literally left and right, but I never thought it would happen to me. I was invincible. Tearing my ACL was a smack in the face.

A few months later, I found myself sitting on the bench, clad in a monstrous leg brace. It is an all too familiar experience. Just three years ago, I found myself in the same spot. Three years ago I did not even make it onto the team.

I always thought sitting on the bench, not playing soccer, would close doors. I found, however, that my "failures" in soccer opened doors for me. My failure to make the soccer team freshman year inspired me to join track to improve my endurance. And my injury before my senior year caused me to fill my summer with research rather than sports. These "failures" introduced me to my passions, passions I would have never discovered.

As I sit on the bench now, I can only wait patiently for what my next "failure" will bring me.

The author of this essay was admitted to Massachusetts Institute of Technology, Class of 2019.

Describe a place or environment where you are perfectly content. What do you do or experience there and why is that meaningful to you?

Today is a good day to push my rock. Every day is. I've had my rock for a while now and with it, I am happy.

I push my rock with all my strength. I shove, I scream, I cry. When gravity pulls it back down, I stomp my feet and call for Mommy, but she doesn't come. I groan and look back at my rock. It looks funny – blue with jagged patches of green, speckled with people. I didn't create it, I found it. Since then, I concentrate on pushing it.

For a moment, the rock grinds to a halt. It looms all around me. I am be surrounded by a dark scowl at my latest burst of excitement in a club meeting, the tired slump of my all-nighter lab buddies, the defeated eyes of my teammate as we lose the badminton match. These are moments of trials and tribulations. These are moments when I realize the rock does not abide by me.

There are rules, laws of the rock, laws that are predefined. They are said to explain everything – from the dark matter of the cosmos to the fourth dimension in quantum tunneling. They draw me in, whispering secrets I long to hear. I cannot bend them to my will, so instead I learn to dance around them. My task is to absorb what I see, and engage with it.

My rock is my undertaking every day, and I am happy.

But not content.

That I achieve only in my bubble.

My bubble is anywhere, at any time. With my rock, I can see where it lacks, where it demands, where it pleads. It beckons to me "I need more, bring more!" So I rush around.

In my bubble, on the other hand, I need nothing more.

There are no rules. There is no master plan. If I want to, I can ski upside down in high heels, in a chocolate desert just two houses down my street. I can stroll through Flatland, taste-testing the doughnuts growing on bushes. I can have hair the color of raindrops.

I am content to drift, in the absence of the image.

A bubble is impossible to buy, construct, or borrow. When I form mine, I may be on a swing, on a plane, in the shower, or in one of many secret places. I won't tell you where, but they are good for bubbles. All I can tell you is that bubbles simply are.

All a bubble requires is my permission, my courage. I play with my energy. I rejuvenate, revive, regrow. In my bubble, I am content.

But not happy.

To be happy is to be engaged with the world, active in discovering and exploring. Content is a fleeting state of anarchy, not intended to solve. There is no debate, no passion that drives. Happy does not live in my bubble.

Happy lives with learning the rock's governing laws, with being able to explain the elegance of natural phenomena, with uncovering truths hidden by fabrics of the universe. It lives with analyzing research data, and having spirited arguments about the validity of scientific journals. It is the study of physics, and its stern perfection.

Yet physics is vast, barely touched by towering stacks of scientific papers. Discovery follows discovery, theory by theory, paradox by paradox. A world that just awaits more probing.

It's all a bit Sisyphean: up and down, up and down, a task that never ends. But by absurdist philosopher Camu's words, the permanence of struggling towards the heights is enough to fill a man's heart. And I agree. Whether I am dancing on top of or being crushed underneath my rock, you must imagine Christina happy.

I will push my rock, climbing to knowledge. I will enter my bubble, to momentarily float in chaos. Then, I will return to my rock, and push.

Happy, content, happy.

MIT Essay #7

The author of this essay was admitted to Massachusetts Institute of Technology, Class of 2015.

1) PHP ----Author

```php
<?php
include_once ("{$siteroot}lib/libqian/includeall.php");
echo<<<AUTHOR
<activity name="web_design" class="pleasure" style="time-
spent:6years;">
<language name="HTML" class="very familiar" />
<language name="CSS" class="very familiar" />
<language name="JavaScript" class="familiar" />
<language name="PHP" class="extremely familiar" />
<language name="SQL" class="familiar" />
<website name="ICT" href="www.tjhsst.edu/~20121qian/ict2011/"
Style="time-spent:1year;" />
<website name="VMT" href="activities.tjhsst.edu/vmt/"
Style="time-spent:2years;" />
</activity>
<script type="text/javascript">
<! --
$LIBQIAN_JS_AJAX;
Ajax = new AJAX() ;
ajax.async() ;
ajax.post ("MIT", {"College Application": "EA"});
ajax.get ("MIT",{"Decision Letter":"December 20, 2011"});
-->
</script>
<noscript>Please enable JavaScript. </noscript>
AUTHOR;
?>
```

2) LIBERTY ----Author

A half-score and two years ago, my family crossed the ocean blue.

Explorers there were before us then, yet we're ecstatic as we flew.

Our landing in America was not as smooth as we had planned:

Our baggage ripped by Customs men, our funding fined for food that's banned.

From Illinois we started off, then went on west for three more years.

We passed through Colorado's peaks, and then returned to Lincoln's heirs.

I started research in NC when I became inspired by

My parents who are physicists, and VA still lets me ask "Why?"

From The Midwest to The East Coast, the expectations are the same:

Good grades only, no bad grades; Math Team, Comp Team, or we're lame.

Our futures all are pre-defined: as doctors, lawyers, CEOs; A wealthy future, wealthy life, fully happy at its close.

But aspirations all aside, we are at our liberties To choose our friends, our clothing, and our transient activities.

My avocations I pursue in my spare time between duties:

I code and program day and night, embellishing websites, beauties.

I study algorithms for the sorting, adding of tree nodes; I write programs to calculate the traffic on imagined roads.

My friends and I compete to pen our stories, poems, works of art.

I think, I muse, I pen it down, then I recite my work from heart.

I'm not only a programmer, but also writer and learner.

I hope that you can see me now as both a poet and coder.

CHAPTER 9

Northwestern University Application Essays

Northwestern University

Evanston and Chicago, Illinois

2015 admission results: 4,912 offers out of 32,060 applicants, 15.3%

2014 admission rate: 12.9%

H.Y. was admitted to Northwestern University, Class of 2017.

Describe a place or environment where you are perfectly content. What do you do or experience there, and why is it meaningful to you?

I am a time traveler. Crazy? Not quite. This technology is not new; in fact it has been around for several centuries now. Jumping from era to era can be tiring, but as long as I have my trusty map to guide my way and snacks to fuel my engine, I am good to go. I still have to drop by the Roaring Twenties – a decade of jazz and cultural explosion. I would love to soak in the live performances of Duke Ellington and Ella Fitzgerald in place of my $20 earphones. I would strut through the New York City streets, lips coated ruby red, bobbed hair sleek against my cheeks, who knows – maybe I would even show a little knee.

Before your lie detector goes off, hear me out. Knowing that I can't physically rewind to the Twenties is certainly not jaw-dropping news. Fortunately, I have discovered my own way of time travel: The Metropolitan Museum of Art, the largest standing time machine in the United States. The Met covers almost every part of the world's history: African, Asian, European, and American. At the Met, my passion to be immersed in the roots of our world is satisfied.

Time rewinds into the late Baroque period in the Rococo rooms at the Met. Anything Rococo looks too sweet to eat like Madison Avenue's Ladurée macaroons. Being surrounded by the creamy pastels and highlights of gold that melt along the graceful curves and corners instantly transform me into a French aristocrat, waiting for my poodle to be pampered and my pillows to be fluffed. In the corner, a fair skinned woman, bathed in sunlight, plucks Handel's Concerto in Bb on the harp. It is hard to understand or feel what I just described without seeing the room, but if you are ever around New York City, I strongly suggest you stop by. I find my peace there, separated from our rapid, technology-crazed society, and relive a simple life 200 years ago full of pure beauty. Inside the Met, I tune into my imagination and it becomes a reality.

Museum trips have been and will always be a part of me. Instead of using words and phrases, world stories are graphically told. At the Met, seeing is believing – and learning.

Growing up, I have always been a visual learner, which is one reason why I love math and music. To me, math is a visual art: real world problems are represented first by translating them into equations using symbols and numbers. Music is made through notes parallel or related to the main key. Arrangements of the same notes churn different emotions.

Throughout high school, history has always been an enigma to me, probably because of the way it is taught. Who said textbooks are the best source of learning history? A forty-minute lecture about the social, economic, or political aspects without "visualizing" any makes me feel lost in the explanations and theories. It is like teaching me everything about music without letting me hear it. At the Met, our ancestors tell their stories through a variety of colors, expressions, and mediums. That is why visiting museums is the best way to satisfy my curiosities about history. So whether I relax and stroll through time, or I actively analyze the past and transport from wormhole to wormhole, each journey is treasured, and I gain something new every time.

As far as time travel goes, who knows if the time machine will ever get invented? I can only hope. If it becomes a reality in my lifetime, I will slip on my flapper shoes at the speed of light and swing by the Jazz Age.

The author of this essay was admitted to Northwestern University, Class of 2017.

When I was very young, perhaps six or so, Baskin Robbins was "the happiest place on Earth." I remember tiptoeing to look in the display glass, growing excited at the sight of each flavor's exotic color, and trying so hard to choose between Chocolate Chip Cookie Dough and Very Berry Strawberry. The lady behind the counter sensed my deliberation (either that, or she was getting impatient), and offered to put both flavors on one cone. The feeling I got? It was Saturday morning cartoons, a twenty dollar bill in the pocket of a winter coat – endlessly content. It's not often in life that one can have all her passions combined.

Upon researching Northwestern's Medill School of Journalism, I was reminded of this perfect combination. At Medill, I could pursue an education in media, journalism, writing, communications – while still integrating myself into the life of Evanston and nearby Chicago.

Academically, Medill offers endless learning possibilities and one of the most unique studying environments in the country. The journalism major not only includes countless in-class lectures, but also hands-on experiences in Northwestern's own technologically advanced filming studios. As the head of my school's Media Group and director for the school's news broadcasts, I'll be the first to admit that working with professional material excites me to no end. At my high school, many cameras are out of service, and the director's booth is only partially functional. The microphones have more sass than I do, and often mute themselves. Although I could watch a 30 minute news segment created wholly (from writing the scripts to editing footage), all the hoops I had to jump through took away from my satisfaction. Medill, however, is an opportunity for me to observe professional teams of news anchors and camera crews in an environment with unlimited capacity. Although I can't roam freely between sound booths and backdrops, just being in those studios would remind me of my beloved Saturday morning cartoons.

But journalism isn't just about what happens on-camera or behind the scenes of a TV station. It's also the painstaking process of writing – of creation. This year, I became vice editor-in-chief of the school magazine. I thought my job would be to look over articles and make sure they were grammatically correct. I couldn't have been more wrong. Ninety percent of the time, I had to completely rewrite the articles. It tested my ability to be informative, concise, and efficient all in one go.

On top of my editing duties, I also had to search for a sponsor when the mag exceeded the school budget. While the problems I encountered in this experience were endlessly trying, the accomplishment I felt when I held the completed editions in my hand was hugely fulfilling. They were solid proof that somehow, I was able to contribute to something greater than myself – something that united a group of people at school purely through the power of language.

This magazine was my way of communicating with the hundreds of other students I didn't share a class with. At Medill, I'd continue to take part in student publications. If I find time, I'll join the staff of both North and Helicon, and try to insert myself into every aspect of Northwestern's journalism life.

Of course, academics won't be the only thing I pursue at Northwestern. I also want to be in the stands during Northwestern's football games, clad in purple and white, cheering on the Wildcats. I'd gather my friends on the rooftops of student dorms during Primal Scream, or sit near the Clock Tower for lunch. I might even quote Kant on the steps of Deering while I struggled to graduate with an IMC Certificate. In Northwestern's beautiful Evanston campus, I rediscovered that combined ice cream cone, the perfection I once thought could only exist in my memory.

Thomas was admitted to Northwestern University, Class of 2019.

"WAKE UP!" my counselor yells. "You'll all be late for morning line up!" I look at my watch. It was 6:33. Still groggy and wondering how I missed Reveille, I frantically search for my shoes and scramble to line up in the front of the cabin with my cabinmates. Before I can fully open my eyes, I hear the second call and sprint to the blacktop and wait patiently for the day's announcements. Afterwards, I drag myself back to my cabin shivering in the fresh morning air. Back in the cabin I check what my morning chore was today. I had toilet duty…

This has been my typical morning for three summers now. While this might sound like hell, Interlochen Center for the Arts is a place where I am perfectly content. Located between two lakes in the deep woods of Northern Michigan, everything is peaceful and serene. Away from the stresses and distractions of living in modern society, Interlochen allowed me to focus on developing my craft as a clarinetist and ultimately an expressive musician. At Interlochen, I experienced collaborating with a community of talented and passionate young artists from all over the world. I studied with world-class faculty who were truly passionate about passing on their love and skills for music to their students. All of these people shared the same passion for music as I did.

Ever since my first summer at the magical place known as "Interlochen", my goal has always been to play in the World Youth Symphony Orchestra (WYSO). I remember being captivated by their passion and energy during performances of Pictures at an Exhibition, The Firebird, and Beethoven's Ninth Symphony among others. This past summer, I was finally presented with an opportunity to achieve that goal – I was admitted to the orchestra program, which means I had a shot for WYSO. However, during the opening week of camp, I bombed my seating audition and was placed in the lower orchestra. Although I had practiced all of the excerpts for hours and hours, my nerves had gotten the better of me. Having only two more auditions left, I started practicing for the next one right away.

Determined to succeed, I went into the audition calm and collected and played the best audition I had ever played. Unfortunately, competition was fierce and ultimately I was placed in the lower orchestra again. Although I moved up and was selected as the principal, I was still extremely disappointed – I was only one seat away from achieving my goal. Being so close but yet so far from my goal, I was feeling discouraged, but supported by my encouraging friends and my teacher, I became even more determined to succeed.

Wanting to do whatever it took to become a member of WYSO, I asked my teacher for his advice. He agreed with me that my audition was technically perfect that I played all the correct rhythms and notes, but he felt it was missing the most critical part – the musical idea. Obsessing over every last technical detail in the music, I had forgotten the soul of music. Those next two weeks alone in the woods, in my favorite stone practice hut, I made sure to always try to convey a musical idea in my playing. And when the day of reckoning finally came, I played like I did in my practice and I finally achieved my goal. I was finally in WYSO!

Interlochen provided me with experiences, friends, and valuable teachings, like the rewards of hard work and perseverance that I will value for the rest of my life. I couldn't imagine receiving any of these benefits anywhere else. The moment I step foot on the familiar Interlochen campus every summer, I smile, knowing the summer ahead of me will be filled with hard work and fun. Interlochen is the place where I am perfectly content.

CHAPTER 10
Princeton University Application Essays

Princeton University

Princeton, New Jersey

2015 admission results: 1,908 offers out of 27,290 applicants, 7.0%

2014 admission rate: 7.3%

Princeton Essay #1

The author of this essay was admitted to Princeton University, Class of 2019.

Recount an incident or time when you experienced failure. How did it affect you, and what lessons did you learn?

"Failure is the mother of success!" It is easy to say, but difficult to practice.

Leaning on my bookshelf is a weathered and worn out frisbee with the words Montgomery Ultimate Frisbee plastered on the front. With every scratch and every dent comes a memory of tossing around with my friends after school, practice at the park on the weekends, and competing at States. While frisbee may seem like nothing more than just a hobby to some people, my time on the field has helped me learn to have a better grasp over my emotions, as well as taught me how to maturely deal with failure.

Spring, 2014. It was finally time for our first game at States. In the first few minutes of the game, I made a good cut in, and caught the disc. Looking up the field, I saw my teammate open, and went for a long huck deep. But I underestimated the distance I had to throw, and the frisbee landed nowhere near where I wanted. As I stared at my throw and berated myself for my poor decision, the other team made a series of quick passes and scored. I looked down the field, and realized I was supposed to guard the player who caught it in the end zone, becoming even more frustrated with myself for letting my emotions affect my gameplay.

Later in the game, I made a long run deep and dove for the frisbee, but fumbled it. Instead of getting up quickly, I slammed the ground and cursed my mistake. During this time, my defender picked up the frisbee and made a long throw I could have easily blocked. Another point against us that I should have prevented.

Eventually, Coach pulled me out of the game. I threw my water bottle to the ground and sulked on the bench. All our expectations for the season had come crashing down. In the end, we lost 13-5.

Looking back, my failure that day wasn't in failing to score more points for the team, or preventing more points from being scored, it was in the breaking the spirit of the game. What really stands out to me about frisbee isn't the flashy plays you can make when laying out for the disc or going for a long huck, but the concept of the "Spirit of the Game." While sportsmanship is not unique to Ultimate, the spirit of the game creates a mutual respect amongst the players and allows for us to referee the matches amongst ourselves themselves. During the game, human nature reared its ugly head amidst high emotions and my "win at all cost" mentality, which caused me to lose sight of one of the most important aspects of the game.

My reactions to my failures proved to be more consequential than my failures themselves. They directly caused my team to concede unnecessary points, and more importantly, embarrassed myself and my teammates. By continuing to dwell on my errors and overreacting in the heat of the moment, I made the situation even worse. Instead, I should have kept a level head and calmly rebounded. Constantly reprimending myself for my mistakes and letting it get in my head in the moment does nothing to help, while analyzing why I failed at a more appropriate time allows me to improve myself in a beneficial and healthy manner. My journey in Frisbee taught me the lesson that failure provides the opportunity for learning and improving! Failure can be as valuable as success, if not more!

Princeton Essay #2 (Common)

The author of this essay was admitted to Princeton University, Class of 2019.

"Where are you from?" asked the old man after realizing I wasn't a local. I was in France for the summer, and making small talk while waiting in line at a restaurant. Thinking that he meant which country I was visiting from, I replied "America". "No, where are you from? Cambodia? Thailand?" Annoyed that my answer was somehow "incorrect", I hastily replied with a simple,"China." However, I couldn't help but wonder why my answer of America was unsatisfactory.

This little exchange raised many interesting questions about myself and my cultural identity I had never thought about in depth before. What does it mean to be from somewhere? Why is it that the expected response, for me at least, that "China" instead of "suburban New Jersey" is where I've grown up? One reason, I imagine, is simply because I look Asian. Indeed, I'd always assumed that being raised in a Chinese household meant that I was Chinese. But does that really mean that I must identify myself as such?

Lying in bed later that night, I reflected on which culture had had a larger impact on myself. Aside from the occasional short vacation to visit my relatives, I have never lived in China, never had any real experiences there. I was born in Chicago, Illinois and spent nearly all my life in central New Jersey. I have been a fan of American entertainment, listening to artists like Imagine Dragons, Kanye West, and The Killers, and watching shows and movies like Breaking Bad and American Psycho. I have been exposed to and adopted ideological principles like individualism, egalitarianism, and a faith in freedom and democracy that, while not uniquely American, are all integral to its culture.

Still, I can't just brush aside my Chinese heritage that easily. If anything, it has helped to enrich my views on the world. For one thing, there is a huge emphasis on familial bonds and caring for the elderly in China. Growing up and living with my grandparents, I thought that this was a common practice and was surprised to find out that it was actually very rare in the United States. At the same time, my Chinese heritage has provided me with a great deal of frustration. The many stereotypes associated with Asian-Americans have created this idea of a "model minority" that, while sounds positive, is anything but. Upon learning that I loved playing the violin, or was a member of our school Science Olympiad team, my peers, more often than not, responded with an "of course," as if to say it was all a result of my "Asian-ness." My personal interest and academic achievements were often marginalized as representative of the Asian American stereotype instead of my own hard-work and genuine passions. When I was younger and more naïve, I didn't think it was such a big deal. But now, I can clearly see that this idea of a "model minority" has impeded upon my search for a personal identity and dulled my individualism, reducing me to nothing more than a cookie-cutter stereotype in the eyes of everyone else.

This issue of cultural identity is not as clear cut as I had previously imagined. My interactions with the old man had prompted me to reevaluate my ideas of who I am. I am of Chinese heritage raised with many of the values of Chinese culture, but I am much more than that. Growing up surrounded by American culture has played a larger role in my identity than where my parents were born. In this multicultural world, the mix of Eastern and Western values blurs racial colors. I cannot say I am Chinese, or that I am American, because it is not that simple. Instead, I can confidently say that I am a Chinese-American from the state of New Jersey.

The author of this essay was admitted to Princeton University, Class of 2019.

Describe a place or environment where you are perfectly content. What do you do or experience there, and why is it meaningful to you? (650 word limit)

My oversized tee-shirt looks like a Jackson Pollock piece, splattered with brilliant reds, yellows, and blues, with its right sleeve unintentionally dipped into the paint on my palette. My arms and hands have taken on lovely rainbow shades as well, sporting vivid splotches that leave little bare skin exposed.

"Alice," my friend Patricia calls from the easel next to mine. I turn just in time for her to smear a paint-covered thumb across my forehead, an addition to my collection of smudges. "Simba!" she says, and I laugh at the Lion King reference.

Patricia and I are among a handful of students who have frequented the Fang-Art Studio since first grade, when we jokingly abbreviated it as "FART" Studio.

Having worked alongside these studio-mates for the majority of my life, I've come to think of them as siblings, and regard the studio as a second home.

"FART" Studio is a lively workspace, perpetually bustling with the sounds of paint rollers squeaking over printmaking boards, charcoal sliding smoothly against paper, pens scribbling down lecture notes, and water slipping through color-stained fingers. It is a place abundant in hearty laughter and thoughtful silence, in critiques and discussions that often last longer than two hours. Among the chatter, excited friends recommend new reads, and Mr. Fang, the studio's mentor, emphatically lectures the principles of design. I remember entering the studio as a simple child who loved to doodle flowers and princesses, and feeling intimidated by Mr. Fang because he gave such straightforward critiques. Since then, I have grown to appreciate his candid speaking style, and to understand that his encouragement of unadulterated feedback enables me to learn from my and my peers' mistakes.

The studio is a place that fosters originality and creativity, a place that challenges me to think outside the box that's outside the box. It is somewhere I will struggle for hours in but never wish to leave. Through grappling with unfamiliar media, I have learned to be confident, to be able to paint a dark streak against a white wall without hesitation, or to cut apart a piece I've worked on for weeks. I have explored the spectrum of artistic styles in search of my own expressive voice, and developed the perseverance to draw until my hands physically ache in the knuckles; I wear the visible marks of my labor – callouses on my fingers and ink stains on my skin – everyday to school. I've found that perseverance, resourcefulness, and curiosity, traits that I value at the studio, expand beyond art: they guide the way I approach daily life, whether I am solving a physics problem, trying to feed my baby cousin vegetables, or capturing a mental snapshot of a peculiarly shaped tree. But most importantly, I've realized that I want art to play a role in my future; I've decided that I want to live and breathe art wherever I go and whatever I do, that I want to create beautiful, conceptual work that will make a difference in whatever career field I pursue.

The studio has encouraged me to take pride in my work and continue with what I love most – art. I love that art can be more than just something aesthetically pleasing: Art can be disturbing. Art can carry messages. Art can touch lives. I love that art comes in so many different forms and that it has the ability to capture such raw emotion. I love that art has the power to both humble and inspire me, that it gives meaning to my life and influences my values. I love that art connects me to others out there who share this same adoration, from across the world to beside me in the studio.

I dip my thumb into the pool of red acrylic on my palette.

"Patricia," I say, grinning as I reach for her forehead.

"Simba!"

The author of this essay was admitted to Princeton University, Class of 2019.

One of the memories I cherish most today is that of a two week-long environmental convention I attended in Daejeon, South Korea while participating in a United Nations Environment Programme organized painting competition. The time that I spent in Daejeon was both informative and exhilarating – I met incredible children from all over the world, peers who cared deeply about protecting the Earth, all congregated in one spot. I was awed by a girl named Cassandra, who founded "Turn Grease Into Fuel", a project focused on creating biodiesel from used cooking oil. A young Indian boy told me that he picked up litter from the beach to make handkerchiefs. I listened to people my age give presentations about a variety of topics ranging from air pollution to zero emissions, and planted a sapling with children from a movement hoping to grow one billion trees. With my hands buried in dirt and feet cushioned by grass, I realized that the connection between humans and the Earth was more tangible than I had ever imagined.

The children at the convention taught me how to love the Earth, and without them, I would never have understood that the UNEP competition represents much more than just an art contest. It relays a message as large as our world, perhaps even bigger. I remember thinking before the convention that reducing environmental impact was as simple as recycling and carpooling, but I recognize now that the scope and intricacy of environmental issues render solutions much more complex. Billions of gallons of potable water are used every week to water American lawns, and significant amounts of fossil fuels are burned every day to produce the food that we eat – and yet, such large-scale problems remain obscure. I am researching to deepen my understanding of these issues, and spreading awareness to my community as an ACE climate leader; I see college as an opportunity to both develop my environmental knowledge and better equip myself to reach out to others.

And although awareness is important, I know that it isn't sufficient if not followed by action. I bike whenever possible. I encourage my parents to buy local produce. I am the founder of my school's Recycled Crafts, a club dedicated to creating artwork from recycled materials. I sent the President a letter once, urging him to attend Copenhagen 15, a worldwide conference dedicated to the issue of climate change. I intend to get involved in grassroots campaigns and environmental activism in college and beyond to inspire others to join the movement. I feel truly lucky to have had attended the Daejeon convention, as it has shaped the person I am today: a girl proud to be tremendously passionate about the environment.

Calvin was admitted to Princeton University, Class of 2019.

Recount an incident or time when you experienced failure. How did it affect you, and what lessons did you learn?

On a hot summer day in 2008, my family visited my great aunt in Nanjing, China. Though I was usually greeted with assorted candies and an affectionate hug, the first thing my great aunt uttered when she saw me was "Wow! You're so fat!" And with a wink and a pinch on my chubby cheeks, she turned to my parents, congratulating them on raising such a strong boy.

I was mortified by her remark, and hurt by her apparent apathy in regards to my prepubescent "feelings". Later on, I learned that in China, calling a loved one fat is not offensive at all. In fact, many elders want their grandchildren to be fat, as it traditionally represents health, happiness and fortune. My mom, however, a 20-year resident of the US and health nut, did not subscribe to the same beliefs. She sprang into action immediately, reading about childhood obesity, showing me the messages, and giving me frequent lectures on how I should put weight loss as my first priority. Although I acquiesced to her points, I was reluctant to change.

Soon after that, I started playing tennis competitively. I joined our high school's varsity tennis team in my freshman year and started playing the first singles in my sophomore year. Despite the fanfare, I turned out to be a total disappointment. Point by point, game by game, I was dismantled by each of my opponents. I did not win a single match the entire season. After losing my last match, I felt shrouded in a cloud of hopelessness and defeat. I had failed my team, my coach, and myself. I was not lacking in skill; the culprit, in my assessment, was being out of shape.

This was a thunderous wake-up call. I felt, for the first time, the intrinsic desire to increase my fitness level. No more was there any self-denial, only the fiery newfound passion that propelled me into actively pursuing my fitness goal. I began to train like a maniac, spending hours per day exercising, embracing the soreness and pain as benchmarks toward my goal. I stopped playing video games, my then favorite leisure activity, and replaced it with hiking, longboarding, basketball, tennis, and gym workout. Moreover, I became keenly aware of the importance of having a well-balanced diet, which I had woefully ignored before. I even started cooking my own and my family's meals to follow dietary recommendations.

My persistent efforts had paid off. After 10 months, by the time the tennis season started this March, I had lost 35 pounds. At 6 feet and 178 pounds, I felt fit and athletic. I enjoyed a stellar season this time, playing first singles, finishing undefeated, placing first in our region, and qualifying for the state-level high-school tennis tournament. After the last match, as I reported my winning score, a profound sense of accomplishment swept over me, a wondrous moment etched in my memory and shared by my ecstatic coach and teammates. Now, another 7 months have passed, I can proudly say that I have maintained my healthy weight and lifestyle and am determined to stay this way to enjoy good health and youthful vitality.

This fitness endeavor, seemingly an added burden onto my busy schedule, has turned out to be most inspiring. It has strengthened my belief that failure can be a stepping-stone to greater success and in this process we can discover our personal potential and achieve the previously unthinkable. Looking forward, the future appears to be bright and exciting but challenges are inevitable. No matter what surprises or pitfalls may pervade the road ahead, I look forward to the journey. My friends and family are my gas tank; their support and belief are my fuel. The lessons and principles I have learned are my guiding lights; the opportunities open to me are my wheels onward. And above all, I am the vehicle toward my own future.

Calvin was admitted to Princeton University, Class of 2019.

Please briefly elaborate on one of your extracurricular activities or work experiences that were particularly meaningful to you. (About 150 words)

I discovered longboarding as a fascinating sport in my sophomore summer and immediately fell in love with it. After dozens of falls, road rash, and abrasions, my longboarding skills quickly improved. The thrill of longboarding is so raw and so volatile; each and every hill has its own challenges, and I am the master of my own speed. I can choose to fly down the hill, feeling the wind stinging my face and ruffling my clothes, or I can slow down, enjoying the precision and ease of movement that a longboard allows. Longboarding is my escape from chaos and my retreat from frenzy. It is my art form and my medium of creative self-expression. Just like the bamboo paper of a Chinese calligrapher or the easel of a Romantic painter, my longboard is my paintbrush. I use longboarding as a form of catharsis, a source of tranquility, and most of all, a vivid reminder of the great joy of living.

The author of this essay was admitted to Princeton University, Class of 2019.

Kitchen = Cooking + Cuisine + Contentment

I sit on a black stool in my messy kitchen, awaiting the beep-beep of the oven. The dishes are stacked but unwashed; a faint mist of flour hangs in the air. Puddles of water, powder and other ingredients decorate the table. Despite my usual perfectionist tendencies, I am unfazed by the disorder. I sit on my stool, inhaling aromas wafting from the warm steel box, feeling tiny speckles of flour settle on my skin, brimming with anticipation for my creation to emerge. I am content.

Baking encapsulates the best and most beautiful in me: an embrace of science as I realize it in the kitchen, a love for the authenticity of the touch and a delight in sharing a piece of my heart.

In contrast to the detached motions of daily life, baking fulfills my scientific fascination for witnessing seemingly magical transformations. In the kitchen, I observe the physical changes of color and texture, the fine cracking of tart crust when baking. Metamorphosis occurs on a chemical level too. The irreversible unfolding of proteins in eggs to give structure to the crust, the caramelizing of sugar in the peach slices in the tart, the changing shades of beige as heat diffuses through pastry. Biological transformations – the shrinking peach as cells become flaccid and membranes loosen, bulging with hot air only to burst and glue to the flesh, the tightening of fibers in the stem as water vaporizes and the growth of yeast creating pockets of air pushing against a gluten film mesmerize me. They signify that my ingredients obey the same fundamental laws as neutrinos in the Hadron collider. Knowledge satisfies the brain, but tiny miracles of the peach tart seduce the soul.

The tactile nature of baking also feeds my contentment. In the classroom, I learn equations of projectiles, flaws in the Treaty of Versailles, theories of the market. I evaluate and analyze decisions and discoveries of others, commenting on the outcome. These abstractions are engaging but untouchable. I am never part of the processes. In the kitchen, however, I feel the weight of flour on my arm, the elasticity of jelly on my fingertips and the softness of the cookie dough on my palm. The touch affirms my participation in the creation. The effort of my muscles proves that I have driven the process. Like craftsman, writers or any who do labor, I too have physically exerted myself. Leaning over the marble, the curved grain of the oak rolling pin does not escape me. I am alive.

Yet the most beautiful aspect of baking is that I can share my creations. When I ask my family to taste the tart, when my mother unwaveringly says, "looks delicious!" without glancing at the mousse, when my brother devours the still hot cake then fans his mouth, I revel in the atmosphere I have wrought. The results vary – delectable pastry, forgotten baking soda, far too much sugar. Beyond awards of smiles, it is the act of giving itself; much more than whether the recipient devours the pastry or feeds it to the cat. At the moment of transfer, my gift is not a cupcake but a culmination of my effort, time and passion. Among the most valuable gifts I can give, it carries a morsel of my soul.

There is yet still a subtle difference. To others, the product is the source of accomplishment – its aesthetics, its taste, its fulfilling of a basic desire. To me, however, the contentment lies in the process. The snippet of time spent baking is a piece of solitude that offers me an opportunity to peek inside and reflect: to understand myself. These distinct points in my linear consciousness of time and space where I sit awaiting the joyful beep-beep of the oven, they whisper: baking – peach tart – contentment. This is you, Kate.

CHAPTER 11
Rice University Application Essays

Rice University

Houston, Texas

2015 admission results: 2,650 offers out of 17,900 applicants, 14.5%

2014 admission rate: 15%

The author of this essay was admitted to Rice University, Class of 2019.

Tick. Tock. Tick. Tock. Time passes relentlessly and my past footprints begin to be obscured by plans for the future – difficult to revisit. For me, there's no place – no hallway, no room, no landscape that evokes my deepest memories. Instead, when music plays, the chords, melodies, and lyrics take me to a former time and place, bringing back all I felt in that moment. Eyes closed, ear-buds in, iPod on. Shuffle.

2003. I was a typical Canadian first grader – tiny, loud, and energetic – except unlike everyone else, I spoke not a word of English.

At school, I escaped my feelings of displacement through my MP3 player, filled with familiar Chinese songs. But somehow, "Once More" by the Crpenters wriggled its way into my playlist. It was astonishingly different – soft, mellow, and wistful – the kind of music played in coffee shops to accompany the pitter-patter of rain. Although I didn't understand its lyrics, I knew its message by heart. The artists' yearning for the past resonated within my own life and "made me smile" inside. The reassurance that my nostalgia wasn't anomalous let me start anew, knowing that "every sha-la-la…still shines" on what I left behind. Word by word, I broke down my language barrier and invited in Western culture. I learned that change was okay - natural even - that moving forward was not synonymous with letting go; it was simply welcoming a new beginning. Shuffle.

2011. 447 of us filled the gymnasium for our eighth grade graduation.

I strutted in with heels too high for my feet, robes too loose for my shoulders, and a grin too large for my face. The graduation video played to the gentle plucking of guitar strings in Taylor Swift's "Never Grow Up." At that time, my greatest challenge was simply entering high school and fighting the sentiment to "just stay this little." But, I put on a brave mask of anticipation – each obstacle an opportunity to prove myself. I "remember the footsteps" I've taken, but at the same time, look onwards toward a future of possibilities. From that moment, I left my comfort zone, determined to challenge myself and achieve. When the song's outro segued into excited chattering between parents and graduates, my next adventure had begun. Shuffle.

2014. It was 4am and a single room was lit in my house.

The stress of junior year had set in and I started drowning in my responsibilities – clawing from one week to the next. Yet, amidst the chaos, I found a warm feeling in connecting with others between the verses of "The Cave" by Mumford and Sons. I had always been independent – afraid and hesitant to meet new people. But when I discovered how easy it was to initiate interesting conversations with classmates, I became unchained from the shadows of my personal cave, wondering what I was so afraid of all along. I realized we were going through similar challenges, and that our hardships were shared. In branching out, I gained not only perspective on my world, but also light on myself. With the help of others, I picked myself up "despite my growing fears" of getting thrown down again, undaunted by adversity. Whenever I hear this bluegrass tune, I smile at how far I've come since high school began. Shuffle. These songs store pieces of my life in a way that physical places simply cannot. My iPod is not just a source of entertainment, but a growing library of my memories. During the intros, montages flash before my eyes and give me the power to time travel – each song a doorway to a distinctive moment. Etched into its hard drive are the lessons I've learned, the values I live by, and the people I hold close. Except this isn't a typical 64GB iPod; my story has no maximum capacity and will continue to expand.

Rice Essay #2

The author of this essay was admitted to Rice University, Class of 2019.

Please briefly elaborate on one of your extracurricular activities or work experiences. (150 word limit)

The summer of 2014, I worked under Professor Maura Boldrini in the Columbia Stem Cell Initiative. Our lab team used immunohistochemistry to analyze Major Depressive Disorder in the context of neurogenesis.

I studied the cell-regulating protein, mTOR, through developing my own protocol, completing experiments, and analyzing results using stereology. I learned professional lab procedures, biological concepts, and abstractions involved in the nebulous disease of depression. Though I have done research in my own synthetic biology club, iGEM, this experience exposed me to many aspects of the professional scientific world. I experienced frustration when tissue shredded during the process of antigen retrieval, realization when the concepts clicked in my head, liberation in the clinking of my first set of slides, and inspiration when I saw my first positive cell.

I hope to contribute to the preservation of the human brain's integrity through safe, effective antidepressants and combat neurodegenerative diseases at large.

With the understanding that the choice of academic school you indicated is not binding, explain why you are applying to that particular school of study. (150 word limit)

It seems we seldom use kinematic equations outside physics class, calculus outside math class, or DNA analysis outside biology class, but engineering brings these concepts together.

When I joined FIRST robotics, I was thrown into the lab. I learned to cut, drill, and wire immediately. I learned to program on the fly. I learned to fix our robot in the mere moments before each match. The spontaneity and energizing atmosphere of build season culminated into our exhilarating final test. The enchanting vitality our robot held propelled me toward more discoveries, toward more exploration.

To me, engineering is a creative outlet. This hands-on experience provides me with a way to challenge myself – thinking and rethinking of solutions to everyday problems. In choosing to study engineering, I choose to learn new ways to think and stretch my imagination, to bring about more technological advancement into the context of social improvement.

How did you first learn about Rice University and what motivated you to apply? (250 word limit)

While scouring through Hugh Herr's TED Talks on YouTube about bionics and prostheses, I came upon a Rice Engineering video – the first time I officially learned of Rice University. This video told the story of Dee Faught, a teenager suffering from osteogenesis imperfecta, a brittle bone disease.

Instead of documenting Faught'disability, this video detailed the opportunity three Rice juniors provided him, in the form of a robotic arm. Unable to reach the ground or turn off a light all his life until now, Faught's newly acquired abilities resulted from just a few semesters of work from these Rice students. In this one video, I saw and instantly clicked with the educational philosophy of Rice University.

Here, students are encouraged to explore their fields, and all the while give back to the community. This is the type of learning environment I wish to immerse myself in, and what most motivates me to apply to Rice. Rice University's heavy emphasis on scientific involvement in the community, whether through the Oshman Engineering Design Kitchen or the Bioscience Research Collaborative, is simply inspirational.

Rice University's partnership with the Texas Medical Center also provides a thoroughly unique research experience. As an undergraduate planning to pursue an eventual career in medicine, this would give me a chance to engage in research both from an engineering and medical point of view. This opportunity –

the opportunity to make a positive impact – is one I wish to experience at Rice University.

The quality of Rice's academic life and the Residential College System are heavily influenced by the unique life experiences and cultural traditions each student brings. What personal perspective do you feel that you will contribute to life at Rice? (500 word limit)

I never experienced the magic of Santa Claus. I reasoned, perhaps reassured myself, that his sleigh could never make it to China and back in just one night. I learned about the tooth fairy in a dentist's commercial. I regarded Thanksgiving a legend only as real as Disney's version of Pocahontas.

After moving to Ontario, it felt so strange writing to Santa Claus in grade one. It was as if all my classmates were under the same collective delusion. When I tried to belie Santa's existence, I landed myself an all-access pass to the principal's office. Instead of building igloos and forts during recess, I listened as he explained to me how I had threatened to ruin the childhoods of twenty some odd kids. So I found myself on the outside of the holiday cheer – not understanding why everyone was so faithful to a lie, yet wanting to be a part of it all.

When I moved to America to start third grade, I tried desperately to fit in. I traded my fried rice and brown noodles for bologna sandwiches and lunchables. I exchanged my chopsticks for forks and knives. I ditched the clothes my grandmother made for sweats from Gap and Justice. In my efforts to fit into Western culture, I had lost what I regarded as my own. I had become an Asian without the flair of heritage and an American removed from its culture.

But all along, I had created my own traditions. Imperceptibly at first, one day's impulsive idea becomes a habit. A habit evolves into a routine. And that routine eventually becomes engrained into my identity. Every Christmas, instead of waking up to Santa's presents under an adorned tree, I wake up to a cup of chai and The Sound of Music with my family. Every Thanksgiving, I attend a potluck filled with 90s karaoke instead of turkey clad in, gravy and cranberry sauce.

Though I seldom have conventional holiday celebrations, I capture the true value behind each – the spirit of family and friends.

Looks like Gordon Bigelow was right all along. Our existence, our experiences and personalized traditions, contributes so much more to our happiness and identity than society's established customs. Adapting to change didn't mean losing myself in a culture, but rather finding my place within one. And if a place didn't already exist, I learned to be fearless in creating my own.

This newfound confidence lets me move forward, without losing the past. In moving forward, I open myself to new traditions – whether they be 3am pizza runs or long nights spent discussing the vicissitudes of life. But without my Chinese birthright, Canadian childhood and American education, I would not be who I am today – a person who has seen, experienced and acknowledged differences in this world. There is no one way to be happy, to learn, or to grow, but there certainly exists a way that I will find for myself, and those around me.

Rice Essay #3 (Common)

The author of this essay was admitted to Rice University, Class of 2019.

Some students have a background or story that is so central to their identity that they believe their application would be incomplete without it. If this sounds like you, then please share your story.

I walked into the offices confused by what I was seeing. To my left, an open door led to shelves of manila folders and volunteers scrambling to pull and file charts. To my right, four ladies sat at a table simultaneously updating patient files and chit chatting. I could hear the loud voice of a woman methodically calling name after name, the clacking of computer keys as volunteers entered data, and the ripping of Velcro as medical students put on and off blood pressure bands. I could only stand and watch as I tried to absorb all of the movements and sounds of the clinic workers. Approximately one hundred patients would walk through the entire process in two hours. All of this organized chaos before the doctors even arrived.

My first day at the free clinic serving the uninsured public, was more than just informational – it was daunting. The clinic was loud, people were impatient, and the waiting patients were often frustrated, but every volunteer loved working there.

After a few months, I had learned all of the skills and jobs a volunteer could do. Immediately after school, I would head to the clinic and begin setting up. I was always the first volunteer to arrive there, which allowed me the time to get to know the patients as well as the many paid employees who organized and ran the clinic. Once the patients began registering, I filled in wherever jobs needed to be done. I could pull patient charts, take their weights, type their information into the electronic database, and direct them along the floor. I always had something to do and was always eager to learn more about the clinic. Although the clinic was only open once a week, I made sure to stay there for as long as I could each day.

Over time, I discovered that Jina, an eighty-year-old Ethiopian woman, and Mina, her daughter, would come in regularly. Because I was at the clinic every week, we saw each other often. Whenever Jina visited, she would immediately light up and wave excitedly. Although she did not know English, she always managed a "hello." Those two wonderful women never complained about the long wait and would just sit patiently by the window. Mina would translate Amharic for her mother, and since the clinic never found an Amharic translator, she would translate for other patients, too. So while her mother waited for the doctors to arrive, Mina helped the other clinic patients with their registration processes. As Mina continued to translate for others, I urged her to begin volunteering at the clinic. Even if her mother did not come for an appointment, I said, she could still translate for the many other Ethiopian patients who came to the clinic. Eventually, Mina began to come every week, inspired to donate her time to the clinic that had supported her family.

Jina began her story at the clinic when she was treated for her malnutrition and anemia. Mina, as well, has finally begun her journey at the free clinic. Every week, I see Mina weaving through all of the other patients trying to deliver charts or find the Ethiopian patient she is translating for. She is the only Amharic translator. Mina constantly meets new people and volunteers, and whenever she interacts with others, I see the helpfulness she offers them. Someday, she too may discover the gratification of not only helping the many patients who walk through the clinic doors, but also through inspiring others to do the same. This experience at the free clinic has truly made a deep impression on me. By gaining an opportunity to help needy patients and recruiting fellow students like Mina involved in the clinic's work, I discovered my passion for building communities – a passion that I plan to carry to college and beyond.

Rice Essay #4

The author of this essay was admitted to Rice University, Class of 2019.

Please briefly elaborate on one of your extracurricular activities or work experiences. (150 word limit)

If you can't touch the bottom in the shallow end and you can't touch the bottom in the deep end, they're the same thing; it's nothing to fear. That's what I told thirty preschool children as they struggled to learn to swim. This was my first time teaching swim lessons and it was a frustrating venture both learning how to teach and applying the lessons. I quickly discovered the necessity of communicating with a caring and positive attitude. If they were scared, I had to be comforting. If they were not moving to their capacity, I learned to push them. They came to camp to enjoy the summer, and I worked hard to make it a memorable event. It would be the summer they learned how to swim. It would also be the summer when I learned a newly found patience – a more nurturing patience.

With the understanding that the choice of academic school you indicated is not binding, explain why you are applying to that particular school of study. (150 word limit)

I have never doubted my love of science. In elementary school, while everybody else would study famous actresses or travelers, I was content with studying Rosalind Franklin, the female researcher who discovered the double helical shape of DNA. Since then, my passion for science has exploded exponentially. Science opens doors to the truth, revealing the foundations of every existence on earth. Every page of a biology textbook, packed with the details of an entire ecosystem or the rungs of DNA, reveals the world. It can explain every muscle movement and machine, and even opens doors to the inexplicable. Science demonstrated to me that discipline and tenacity are virtues. Rice's Weiss School of Natural Sciences offers me that opportunity to venture deeper into the world of science and continue my journey toward understanding.

How did you first learn about Rice University and what motivated you to apply? (250 word limit)

Learning should be a lifelong journey. My parents instilled in me a value for rigorous academic standards that I have maintained throughout my educational journey from elementary to graduation from high school. Rice's reputation as an undergraduate university has stood out in my discussions with counselors and teachers. The university's strength in an interdisciplinary curriculum offers a unique perspective both in the classroom and in the real world. The curriculum reinforces my own values and desire to become a physician and engage with the world in a more expansive basis. The Language and Culture of Medicine and Health Care, combines my own love of the Spanish language and its practical application to medicine. Rice will not constrain my approach to medicine, but will free me to encounter new opportunities and establish new boundaries. The Rice/Baylor Medical Scholars Program provides foundational studies and leads to a more expansive study in medicine.

Medicine is not a myopic study but rather an expansive opportunity to engage the world. I can debate the ethical controversies in Ethics, Medicine, and Public Policy, promote health and well-being in Medical Anthropology of Food and Health, and help interpret Spanish at the Texas Medical Center in the Language of Medicine Practicum II. Rice can connect me to my community with a greater purpose of serving and shape me into a well-rounded, globally literate physician I aspire to become.

The Committee on Admission is interested in getting to know each candidate as well as possible through the application process. The following essay question is designed to demonstrate your writing skills and facilitate our full appreciation of your unique perspective. The quality of Rice's academic life and the Residential College System are heavily influenced by the unique life experiences and cultural traditions each student brings. What personal perspective do you feel that you will contribute to life at Rice? (500 word limit)

I have never truly celebrated an American holiday with my family. When I was younger, Santa Claus was merely an old man dressed in red who stood in store windows and handed gifts to children. I never received gifts because my parents disliked the notion of a single day that seemed focused on materialism. Instead, they preferred to focus on the importance of the gift of family. On Thanksgiving, I never had a turkey with all the trimmings, cranberry sauce, and pumpkin pie for dinner. Although we celebrated with friends, our celebration was never the picturesque scene that appears on every magazine cover. Halloween, Fourth of July, and New Year's Eve were similar. Although we occasionally ventured out and watched the fireworks or the countdown, our celebrations were never grand spectacles. I never resented the fact that I never experienced stereotypical holiday traditions. Instead, I would decorate eggs for Easter, watch the Fourth of July fireworks, and attend Thanksgiving dinners with all of my friends.

My friends offered me a window into a wide range of cultures. I was not restricted by the traditions of my parents, but rather, I was introduced to the spectrum of beliefs, religions, cultures, and traditions of the people around me. I cooked kosher meals with my Jewish friends, attended mass with my Catholic friends, and ate traditional curry with my Indian friends. Through these experiences, I learned to be open minded and accepting of all the people around me. I saw the world around me as an open book filled with friends and acquaintances who could teach me about the traditions that I myself did not celebrate.

Because Rice prides itself on its diversity and inclusion, I can see myself fitting in well. Rice cultivates a diverse community and celebrates the differences in its students, and my own open mindedness about the people around me compliments such a viewpoint. Not only can I pursue an education thoroughly focused on my academic interests, but I can also enjoy a community rich in varying beliefs and cultures. At Rice University, I can grow a fine mind and open heart, ready for the real world.

CHAPTER 12
University of California, Berkeley Application Essays

University of California, Berkeley

Berkeley, California

2015 admission results: 13,330 offers out of 78,923 applicants, 16.9%

2014 admission rate: 18%

UC Berkeley Essay #1 (Personal Statement)

The author of this essay was admitted to University of California, Berkeley, Class of 2017.

Describe the world you come from – for example, your family, community or school – and tell us how your world has shaped your dreams and aspirations.

The Little Mouth That Could

My mouth. It's a trouble maker.

Back in third grade, I was the first girl in class to get braces. They represented every inconvenience possible for an eight year old. I would wake up with a dry mouth, get countless ulcers, be forbidden from chewing Dubble Bubble...all because this mouth couldn't be orderly and obedient. As I sat watching a movie, saliva would drip from my lip corners. In school, friends kept a safe distance when I started talking. "Thpray" was my middle name. I hated my mouth. That year, I started talking less in class, and became a quiet girl, placed on the periphery.

Fast forward six years. The braces were finally coming off, and I lived in a brand new city – Shanghai. It was my opportunity to recreate my image – with a much more wholesome mouth. Freshman year, I gradually became a talker, giving the occasional input on Captain Yossarian's life dilemma, or answering questions pertaining to frictional force. I joined the school's debate team, anxious to test out my new-and-improved speaking skills. It was a blast. The team would often stay together after dinner, discussing the merits of warning labels on foods, or cringing at the side-effects of performance-enhancing drugs. Speech – and all things associated with it – quickly became my greatest hobby.

In tenth grade, my main extracurricular included debate and MUN. These were activities where I could stand in front of a group and just talk. For the first time, I felt that people cared what I had to say. They would ask why I supported strict border control in Kuwait to limit small arms trade, or what the greatest barriers were to achieving the Millennium Development Goals. I even participated in several speech competitions. The feeling on stage was liberating, and I felt the shackles of elementary school embarrassment disintegrate under bright spotlights.

By my junior year, teachers were having a hard time getting me to stop moving my mouth. I remember once in IB TOK class, Mr. Lundberg had drawn a timeline on the whiteboard. My mouth immediately opened.

"If time is the fourth dimension, how can we portray it linearly?" Mr. Lundberg turned around, exasperated.

"It's just a model, Angela."

That day, I realized trying to achieve a balance in the amount of speaking was quite a dilemma. Too little of it, and I might fade into the background; too much of it was painful for others. But with a little bit of the third-grade me, and an equal dosage of high school me, perhaps I'd finally strike the right balance.

To this day, the fast vibrations of my vocal chords and the clicking of my tongue have not yet brought me greatness. I still haven't won the Best Delegate award in MUN, or attended a national debate competition. Occasionally, this mouth will even let loose some spray again.

My mouth. It'll never stop being a troublemaker. But what would I be without it?

UC Berkeley Essay #2 (Personal Statement)

Matthew was admitted to University of California, Berkeley, Class of 2019.

Describe the world you come from – for example, your family, community or school – and tell us how your world has shaped your dreams and aspirations.

Connecting the Dots

Inside the power rack is where I feel most natural, even though there's a couple hundred pounds of weights dangling over me. Before I begin my first repetition of squats, I take a huge breath to build intra-abdominal pressure, a method used to reduce injurious compressive forces on the spinal disks. In plain English, all I did was breathe deeply and hold the breath. But when I was first taught to do this, my instinct was to ask "Why?" It was this initial curiosity about weight lifting that developed into my fascination with biology and anatomy.

My journey to the power rack began after the freshman year basketball season. I was anxious to become a better player for next season so when my knees started hurting I shrugged it off and continued practicing with the pain. The overtraining ended up forcing me to leave the school's basketball team. I was angry with myself because the reason that put me in that position was that I wanted to work hard. I was sparked to learn everything about Jumper's Knee after I was diagnosed with it. The explosive, sudden movements in basketball that caused my knees to hurt led me to try a more controlled form of exercise that emphasizes technique and safety – weight lifting. Even though it was initially only used to supplement my physical therapy, I came to love the activity. This hobby gradually became ingrained into my lifestyle. My parents worried that all my after-school time invested in weight lifting would impede my academics.

Before I began weight lifting, science was just another class to endure. I would get distracted easily and instead of picking an interesting topic for the science fair, I settled for an easy one. Ever since I started lifting weights, I became more interested in the body and its functions. During biology, the unit on molecules (carbohydrates, proteins, and lipids) gave me valuable insight into weight lifting

120

particularly when we discussed the structure and functions of glycogen, a source of energy stored in the muscles. The cramps and soreness that I got from weight lifting became a lot more interesting once we learned about lactic acid

fermentation and anaerobic respiration.

In the setting of the weight room, I have gone through a countless number of experiments, each with its own independent variables, dependent variables, and repeated trials. For every exercise, I adjust the amount of weight, repetitions, rest time, and sets so that I progressively become stronger. This approach led me to think of weight lifting and science as two interconnected disciplines.

Hypertrophy.Ketogenesis.Supination. In the beginning, I had no idea what these terms meant, but I eventually incorporated them into my vernacular. Now I know that the "deep breath" I took while squatting is more precisely called the Valsalva maneuver – named after a 17th century anatomist, and is used to keep the body's core tight in order to brace the spine against a heavy load.

Like most of my peers, there were more than a few times when I dragged myself out of bed and later stared at the clock waiting for the class to end. But through the outlet of weight lifting, I became more energized to learn. Weight lifting didn't waste my time; instead it made me more efficient by changing my attitude and mindset towards learning. My parents have come around as well and are happy with my grades and wellbeing. I never expected two seemingly distant topics to be intertwined with one enhancing the other just like a symbiotic relationship.

Through this journey, I have learned that everything in life can be related back to the classroom, which is why I strive to put forth the same amount of effort in the classroom as I do in the weight room.

The author of this essay was admitted to University of California, Berkeley, Class of 2019.

Describe the world you come from — for example, your family, community or school — and tell us how your world has shaped your dreams and aspirations.

Growing up in a bilingual, immigrant household has shaped me into diverse individual with a broad world view. Both of my parents grew up in rural districts and experienced the Cultural Revolution. They wanted me to have the exact opposite childhood so they raised me to have an insatiable curiosity and passion for learning.

While other kids were playing with their Nerf guns or Gameboys, my eyes were stuck to the television screen where I watched a scientist with a monotonous voice dip various strips of paper in the litmus pH test. At the age of five or six, I could barely comprehend what the man was saying, but I still enjoyed watching the episodes on the VHS tapes in the same sense as reading a picture book. Even though my parents were new to parenting and their new home, they put in a lot of effort to ensure that I wouldn't miss out on the fun typical American childhood activities. During the summer nights, when the sunset well after eight at night, my father would take me to the neighborhood playground. While I played on the swings, he would ask me questions like "What's the state bird of Virginia?" or "What's the state capital of Texas?" and often times I wouldn't know the answer, but he knew that and would then proceed to tell me the answer. My parents were constantly giving me opportunities to explore and learn. They bought me my first Lego set when I was only three, but it was the really large foam blocks. As I got older, my parents continued to supply my appetite for new and challenging Lego sets. When I was ten my parents bought me two containers with many small compartments so I could sort my pieces by color and size for my own projects. I wasn't raised in what most people would think of as "traditional Asian parenting". As I grew older, my parents gave me more freedoms with the inexplicit responsibilities that was attached. They never pushed me towards a certain sport, musical instrument, or subject. I learned to make decisions for myself at an earlier age than most of my peers and that has given me the ability to think for myself. I know what is best for me and what I am interested in. Now, the activities that receive my time and effort are honest passions of mine.

Over the years, when people asked me "What do you want to be when you grow up?" I would usually reply with "Zookeeper!" or "Firefighter!" but with more time to try new activities, now I know that what I truly want to do is be an inventor. The world will always have room for new technology to come in and revolutionize a particular activity. What fuels the fire within me is the satisfaction of looking at the finished product, but more importantly reflecting on the challenging, but fun, creation process. I truly believe in the phrase, "the possibilities are endless" and I hope to expand my bounds by delving deeper in the direction of my passions in a place that will provide me the right opportunities.

CHAPTER 13
University of Chicago Application Essays

University of Chicago

Chicago, Illinois

2015 admission results: 2,365 offers out of 30,192 applicants, 7.8%

2014 admission rate: 8.4%

University of Chicago Essay #1

The author of this essay was admitted to University of Chicago, Class of 2019.

Why University of Chicago?

When I visited UChicago this January, I was skeptical. I had heard countless rumors saying that this place was where "fun comes to die," and being just a teenager, I was certainly not ready for that. However, my reservations were quickly put to rest when I was able to talk to some students there. The student led campus tour made me instantly fall in love with UChicago.

I am not ashamed to admit that I love to ask questions and learn new things. A geeky amusement runs through my body whenever I come across something particularly interesting. I believe UChicago can satisfy my hunger for knowledge. I love the core curriculum because it really makes for a strong, well rounded person and cultivates a critical and creative intellectual capacity that I can rely on long after college. Ultimately, however, my goal is to be able to find a job that I would love to spend the rest of my life doing. My friend who just graduated from UChicago told me how Chicago Careers in Business is a great opportunity and has a high success rate. This program is very attractive to me; it would be something to work towards if accepted to the university.

I started to develop an interest in economics last summer after a Virtual World Experiments in Economics internship sponsored by Nobel laureate Dr. Vernon Smith. We were trained to design and implement economic experiments using a high level of math and programming, which I strongly pursued in and out of high school. Last fall I took the only economics course offered at my high school and found that economics is both scientific and practical. I feel it is the field where I can apply everything I've learned at my STEM focused high school. I also attended the annual meeting of the American Economic Association in Chicago this January and was absolutely fascinated by the breadth and depth of research topics economists presented there. In fact, it was on my trip to this conference that I first visited UChicago. Its rigorous academic programs and the fact that the economics department has numerous Nobel winning professors made me feel that attending UChicago can definitely help me in my pursuit of economics. Not only are the professors more than qualified, they seem to be easily accessible and care about students rather than just their own research. Having no classes taught by TAs is just another testament to the first-rate education provided by the university.

The University of Chicago obviously provides stellar academics, but I am also drawn to the people that I met on campus. These are some of the most quirky, intellectual, friendly, and hardworking people I have ever met. The residence hall system just adds more to the strong sense of family at the university. The house system, as well as the entire campus itself, has a splash of Hogwarts which is definitely another plus. People always tell me that if I was able to enjoy Chicago in January weather, then I must really love it. I fully intend on utilizing all the resources that the university as well as the city of Chicago has to offer. With all of its fun traditions like dollar shake days, the University of Chicago is definitely not where fun comes to die.

The author of this essay was admitted to University of Chicago, Class of 2019.

In the spirit of adventurous inquiry, pose a question of your own. If your prompt is original and thoughtful, then you should have little trouble writing a great essay. Draw on your best qualities as a writer, thinker, visionary, social critic, sage, citizen of the world, or future citizen of the University of Chicago; take a little risk, and have fun.

What is the solution to the currently high unemployment rate in the United States?

High unemployment with a large trade deficit is one of the most pressing issues in America today. With sluggish economic growth, unemployment is constantly on the minds of the American people, especially during the current presidential election. How can we reduce trade deficit and put more Americans back to work? As I watch the news and listen to the presidential debates, many people, including Governor Romney and President Obama, seem to be in favor of putting in trade barriers to keep jobs in the US. Is this really the best solution? Not from what I've learned. Trade can make everyone better off – it is not like sports where one side wins and the other side loses. Countries benefit from trading with one another because trade allows for specialization in productions that countries can do best and have comparative advantages in.

This raises the question of what we should specialize in. Should we be fighting to get menial labor back to America? Do Americans really want low level, repetitive and labor-intensive assembly factory jobs? No, we should not be competing for cheap labor and repetitive work, but competing for and specializing in producing high quality goods and advanced technologies. We need to be leaders in innovation and technology development so we can produce high quality products at a low cost, which we can export to ultimately reduce our trade deficit and unemployment rate.

How can we achieve that? I believe that one way to improve upon the current industrial production system would be to invent and produce a full industrial workforce of robots. They can be used to replace cheap labor and repetitive work altogether. American jobs that cannot be easily outsourced to other countries would be created for the invention, production, maintenance and management of the hardware and software aspects of the robots using US patented technologies.

This idea initially arose a few years ago when my dad took me to the Mercedes-Benz auto plant where he was working, and explained to me their system of detecting defections. The robots they used, while impressive, lacked intelligence and finesse. A few years later after being introduced to new technologies such as Microsoft Kinect and Apple's Siri, I began to realize that these US patented modern technologies could definitely be incorporated into the robots to improve the efficiency and quality of industrial production.

Admittedly, my idea nearly hints at science fiction, but much of the technology we have today was all thought to be impossible just fifty years ago. I'm imagining our nation with a strong presence of robots like in the 2004 movie "I, Robot", except the robots add to the productivity of society and not to the creepiness. Contrary to popular belief, I believe producing robots for our workforce can reduce the unemployment rate and increase the competitiveness of the United States. After all, technology is ever changing, so it never hurts to dream big and hope to change society on a global scale.

University of Chicago Essay #3

The author of this essay was admitted to University of Chicago, Class of 2017.

Spanish poet Antonio Machado wrote, "Between living and dreaming there is a third thing. Guess it. "Give us your guess.

Between: (preposition) expresses the location at, into, or across the space separating; indicating a connection or relationship

Living is established in reality, a constant reminder of human limits – the impossible, the unfeasible – all exist in this state. Dreaming is a mind's ability to extend into fantasy, where these limitations can be overcome. The prompt implies that living and dreaming are two separate entities, completely different, each with their own identity in time and space. However, what lies "between" these states of mind, as shown by the definition, can either be a barrier dividing the two, or a medium synthesizing them. So what both divides and connects living and dreaming?

Writing.

Writing allows people to pay homage to their realities by existing in the pantheon of the infinity – somewhere fantastic, beyond the borders of life. I've always been a firm believer that the creation of literature is man's road to immortality. An author can pen his pondering in the only reality he knows, but his mind can travel to any moment of time. With every drop of ink on parchment, his identity is solidified. The feelings he cannot communicate to his world, he can communicate to the paper. This author's words will take on a life of their own. They'll travel past their creator's memories, beyond his death, and into another life. His soul, though based in reality, has found a home in fantasy. When his writing is read, the author has traversed and surpassed the boundary between living and dreaming.

I remember the first time I read Hunter S. Thompson's Fear and Loathing in Las Vegas. I traveled alongside his words, as if I were a part of his mind and the creation process of his characters: Raoul Duke and Dr. Gonzo. I followed their journey into the "heart of the American Dream." Transported back to 1970s Las Vegas, my surrounding classmates became the lizards of a drug-induced hallucination, my chair the plush leather seat of a cruiser coasting past Nevada's deserts. As Mr. Thompson put his experiences into text, he bared his soul, and caught himself in that magical in-between of living and dreaming. In that moment, Thompson was immortal.

Perhaps that is why I have always loved English class. It allows be to become absorbed in another person's mind, suspended in a distant history. Yet in literature, I am still able to interact with my world; see it through the distorted insanity of Don Quixote, or the quiet pondering of Sadegh Hedayat. Focused on this writing that defines more than a person, but also a time, a moment, and a fantasy, I've found the space between living and dreaming.

The author of this essay was admitted to University of Chicago, Class of 2019.

Barbed wire. Iron bars over the windows. "This used to be a prison," our teacher says. Not what I thought I'd picture when I hear the words "perfectly content." What an ideal place for an elementary school, fenced in and locked up. But tucked away, kicking their feet happily under miniscule desks, hidden behind these peeling walls, are the healthy organs in the failing body of inner-city schools.

Fresh off a three hour bus ride from a school that was a lifetime away from these precious children, my peers and I were there to conduct an art lesson. Our chapter of the National Art Honor Society did this every year, picked a low-income school with no art program, wrote a lesson plan, scrounged up the supplies, and went to volunteer. This year we'd come equipped with watercolors, black ink, and miniature paint rollers.

The excitement on their faces when they saw us, the rapt attention they paid to our lesson – stilling restless knees and tapping feet – what they felt can only be described by a character in Chinese, le, which means something like sheer, indescribably pure happiness. That character – a conduit from emotions to words – the look that shone from their eyes and grabbed me by the throat. They bent studiously over their art and I paused to remember this: the rhythmic snick-snick of the rollers in the ink ticking like a metronome, the children's happy gurgling laughter lingering somewhere in between the beats. Later I handed out snacks and fragments of my petted heart to these kids and in return – the quick press of dainty rosebud lips against my cheek, an unforgettable lesson learned on the profoundly intimate, profoundly human principle of giving from your whole being, a tiny handprint in cheeky yellow boldly imprinted on my comfiest pair of sweatpants. It's been six months and I still haven't found the heart (lessness) to wash it out.

An orphanage in Peru with no running water save for the babbling brook of excited children's chatter: same story, different characters. A little girl named Valerie pushing pidgin Spanish through the gaps in her baby teeth, the Jacq-syllable that starts off my name disagreeing with her tiny button of a tongue so that she called me "Lina, Lina, tu eres bonita." Miguel lost his tooth in an intense but short scuffle of a soccer game. I scrabbled around on my knees looking for the tiny pearl thing in the grass and found instead a pearl, in the shallow depths of my whorled seashell heart, of iridescent absolute content. Privilege? I might not have them all but I do live in a house, have teachers who aren't students trekking from the nearest university, running water, and parents who'll drive me half an hour to get KFC on an indulged whim when these kids were gobsmacked at the feast of fried chicken we'd bought them. These little kids laughing with open mouths and crinkled eyes humbled me, filled me with gratitude so acute that if I wasn't already on my knees, breathlessly laughing, wheezing, winded-a young boy on my back dangling his knobby tanned knees off the side, little fist clenched in my hood, demanding I get up and race – I probably would've fallen to them, involuntarily.

Once when I was little, I'd cried because I'd only gotten 14 presents for Christmas and in Harry Potter Dudley had gotten 34, but no material object has ever contented me, made me ecstatic, waxing euphoric, glowing, babbling joyfully, the way a short opportune brush with these amazing kids and their infinite potential, had. It sounds like a line in a pretentious poem – Siken perhaps – define: happy, but here is my definition anyway, cobbled together from paint splatters, grass stains, dirty knees and gap toothed grins, tiny hands and bright giggles: emotional fulfillment so intense one experiences catharsis of the purest order.

Jacqueline was admitted to University of Chicago, Class of 2019.

Beyond your impressive academic credentials and extra-curricular accomplishments, what else makes you unique and colorful? We know nobody fits neatly into 500 words or less, but you can provide us with some suggestion of the type of person you are. Anything goes! Inspire us, impress us, or just make us laugh. Think of this optional opportunity as show and tell by proxy and with an attitude.

The first memory I have of her is when I tried to kill her.

Granted, I didn't know what I was doing; all I knew was that there was this… new creature, barely arm's length, with a spiky cap of black hair and apple cheeks, and she was squalling loudly. I trundled inquisitively over to her quilted basket; she looked back up at me, crossed her eyes in displeasure, and wailed all the more loudly. Equally put out, I grabbed the edge of her quilt with pudgy fingers and pulled it up to cover her tiny snub nose, hoping – or so I assume now – to muffle her screams. Alerted by the siren howls, my panicked mother skidded down the stairs and shooed me away from the bassinet, and thus, sulkily as only a two-year-old can be, I retreated back to my own playpen, wholly disenchanted with baby sisters.

We are too close in age for me to ever have taken on a third-parent role – but when we were toddlers, she idolized me, held my word as gospel truth. How surprised I was, then, to find that she would wind up teaching me, the older by one year and eight months, some of the most vital lessons of my sixteen years; wordless aphorisms written in her fingerprints across my heart. Sure, I taught her how to fly a kite, how to snip off Barbie's long hair, how to multiply by 3s, butthese little things are no match for the indelible mark her unapologetic individuality, her brash confidence, have left on me. She doesn't apologize for her passions, her soaring dreams; by her proxy I've learned that it's okay that I babble endlessly about Kazuo Ishiguro and Oscar Wilde and John Keats, that I want to win the Nobel Prize in Literature. It's totally acceptable that I push the coffee table up against the couch so I can flail crazily around in the family room, speakers blasting Korean pop. It's completely tolerable that I sing loudly and horrifically, mangling poor Adele until our mother pokes her head around the stair banister and asks if it's the tea kettle shrieking or me. I was supposed to grow up faster and set an example, walk in front and clear the path on the road ahead, but I doubled back, borrowed some of her confidence and let it seep into my bones until I was comfortable in my own skin.

Watching her, this girl who is so unflinching in the face of an often cruel world, so shielded against its harsh blows, I realized that in order to truly be confident, I had to embrace myself wholly, every curve, every rough edge. Because of my sister I know to not be afraid to take risks, to not depend on other people's opinions of you, to not be afraid to dream bigger than the ceaseless boundaries of an infinitely creative mind.

And from the day I met her, I've been ceaselessly enchanted with the world.

CHAPTER 14

University of Pennsylvania Application Essays

University of Pennsylvania

Philadelphia, Pennsylvania

2015 admission results: 3,697 offers out of 37,276 applicants, 9.9%

2014 admission rate: 10.0%

UPenn Essay #1 (Common)

The author of this essay was admitted to University of Pennsylvania, Class of 2018.

The sounds of pounding feet and high pitched voices echoed throughout the wood-floored room to a backdrop of piano music. I stood with bated breath at the corner of the room, cupping Nathan's neck and straddling his body from behind. "Hello Nathan, we're glad you're here today!" The children's singing infused the air with excitement as it called for our presence. Together, we tiptoed to the stage and started to stomp and march. As the music dissolved, I watched Nathan's face grow into a smile, a smile that burst with joy and encouraged me to continue my endeavor.

I never thought my passion for dance would be so intimately tied to Nathan, a tiny 10-year-old disabled child. Through the years, from performing ballet at studios to choreographing modern dance at school, I worked hard to convey what makes dance so special to me. I love dance, a true expression of my life, which brings me enjoyment and confidence. Nevertheless, I didn't fully appreciate dance until I became involved in Dancers with Disabilities, a program designed for disabled children to enjoy movement and creative self-expression.

I remember meeting Nathan the first time a year and half prior. "I…I am …uh…Nathan," the boy whispered to me, clinging to his walker with a tilted head and stiff limbs. Perhaps it was instinct, but my aspiration to nurture the vulnerable child flourished at that moment. In retrospect, that was the beginning of an incredible journey for me.

Nathan's disability in movement was presented as the first obstacle in initiating our dance. I distinctly recall my anxiety about the prospect of dancing with a disabled child in a unique way – hands under his head, half the time, to facilitate free movement. For those stressful moments, I struggled to anticipate Nathan's steps, while carefully supporting and navigating him to coordinate his tilting head with brandishing arms. Despite my highest level of concentration, I was terrified. My usual joy for dance was gone, replaced by a deep tension. However, I continued on by lifting Nathan backwards and forwards from corner to corner. Undertaking such adversity was a petrifying experience, but I learned it was the optimal way to grow and change. Looking back, I am grateful of the experiences towards those early days.

Dancing with a physically disabled child can never be easy, but Natha's intellectual limits confronted me with an even greater challenge. I was stretched to my limits when Nathan lay down on the floor, refusing to dance. For a while, my inability to battle this dilemma constantly frustrated me. Rather than capitulate, I learned to read his moods and acclimate myself to different circumstances. Had I observed Nathan slightly perk up, I would have encouraged his arms into a windmill motion, gradually gearing him towards the interest of dance. If it appeared too difficult for Nathan to correspond to the song's cadence, I would have adapted to accommodate his style of erratic motions to encourage him to continue moving. "How about storytelling, instead?" would have skated through my mind if Nathan were disgruntled with his eyes tightly closed, but only as a last resort.

"Was Nathan…Nathan good?" As we left the stage, Nathan gazed at me. "Yea Nathan, you were great!" I grinned, beaming with pride.

What started as assisting disabled children in dance has turned into a journey that shaped a tremendous portion of who I am today. Whether it is mentoring the disabled children's motor skill or promoting their self-expression, whenever I am surrounded by the children who trust me, whom I care of, I find myself fueled with love and encouragement to embrace the bright future, a future for me and for the children.

My journey defines my inner strength that will carry me through my life.

The author of this essay was admitted to University of Pennsylvania, Class of 2018.

Thousands of cells dancing in an array of luminescent colors captured my fascination as I pressed my eyes up against the immunofluorescence microscope. I was enthralled by their nature of being tiny, almost invisible components, yet serving as the basis of all organisms on the planet. After months of working on a project to preserve cellular structures, I found that my life was intimately connected to the cells – their survival bolstered my happiness and their destruction drove my frustration.

I first recognized my inclination towards science when I was a ninth grader, winning an award from a regional Science and Engineering Fair (SEF). Since then, my love for science has been greatly amplified. I pursued my passion beyond the classroom by participating in various extracurricular activities. Working at research labs enlightened me because I gained hands-on experiences and the opportunities to engage in life-changing projects. At Penn – more than anywhere else – I know I will receive the best research-based education because of its world-renowned professors and cutting-edge research opportunities. I aspire to study the neurobiology of schizophrenia and autism under the mentorship of Professor Siegel at the Department of Psychiatry, an opportunity that is currently available at the Center for Undergraduate Research and Fellowship. This area of study, particularly autism, intrigues me because of my real-life experiences with autistic children in dance classes. Their difficulties in following directions and expressing thoughts often impaired my ability to assist them in movement; however, this unique challenge motivated me to discover the cause of the disorder and explore new treatment options.

Beyond the health sciences, I would like to augment my studies with mathematics, computer science, and linguistics through the interdisciplinary major Cognitive Science offered at Penn's College of Arts and Sciences. In my experiences, I find that synthesizing seemingly distinct pieces of knowledge can promote inquisitiveness and strengthen enthusiasm for learning. This is especially true of my dance. My awareness of the limited therapeutic benefits of dance provoked my intellectual curiosity, unexpectedly furthering my interest for science. In my life, my expedition into science is the leap, a favorite movement of choreography. I wish one day, tour jetés, barrel turns, and others will culminate into one piece of dazzling motions that will fulfill my dreams. During college, I want to explore broadly and focus on what matters most to me. Penn is where I will have the best opportunity to delve into those fields.

Besides my academic engagements, I also enjoy supporting the research interests of others through my involvement in SEF. Serving as a judge at a school science fair last year, I found service-oriented activities to be particularly rewarding. By asking the students questions and offering my suggestions, I realized that I can help them and gain an eye-opening experience simultaneously. Now, as Coordinator of the Elementary Outreach program at the Student Advisory Board of SEF, it is my mission to promote students' enthusiasm for science by mentoring and challenging them. At Penn, I look forward to reinforcing these experiences by being involved with programs such as Science in Elementary and Middle Schools, an Academically Based Community Service (ABCS). I aspire to become an integral part of the program.

At Penn, my aspirations will be realized in this challenging, research-integrated environment. In return, I believe the combination of my academic commitment and enthusiasm for the community will unequivocally contribute to the University. My visit to Penn last summer has only solidified what I already know – Penn is an incredible intellectually-stimulating community.

Strolling on Locust Walk, listening to the sound of laughter, and imagining a day examining microscopic organisms, I know I will thrive in this climate. This is the place with a rich, vibrant culture that will push me to my limits, let me meet like-minded students, and still give me moments of peace.

Selecting Penn as my college of choice only seems natural.